STRIKES – A DOCUMENTARY HISTORY

By the same authors —

1868 — Year of the Unions
The History of British Trade Unionism
   — *A Select Bibliography*

STRIKES
A DOCUMENTARY HISTORY

R. and E. FROW and MICHAEL KATANKA

CHARLES KNIGHT & CO. LTD.
LONDON
1971

Charles Knight & Co. Ltd.
11/12 Bury Street, London EC3A 5AP
Dowgate Works, Douglas Road, Tonbridge, Kent

Printed in Great Britain by
A member of the Brown Knight and Truscott Group

SBN 85314 110 X

STRIKE SONG

Come Mary put mi pit clogs by,
From th' jacket shake the dust,
We've gone on strike for ten per cent.;
We'll get it lass, I trust.
There's nothing cheers a house so much
As a bright fire o' coal,
Yet colliers' wages scarce will keep
The body with the soul.

    But we're on strike for ten per cent,
    We're not down-hearted yet,
    We are on strike for ten per cent,
    And ten per cent we'll get.

Don't bother much o'er food for me,
But give eawr Joe enough.
If he and thee get decent meals,
I will put up with rough.
And cheer thee up mi bonnie lass,
And little Joe don't fret,
That dobbi-horse I promised thee,
When th' strike is o'er theay'll get.

    For we're on strike for ten per cent,
    We're not down-hearted yet,
    We are on strike for ten per cent,
    And ten per cent we'll get.

MARY THOMASON, *Warp and Weft – Cuts
from a Lancashire loom* (1938)

Contents

Contents

Introduction

FOR over two hundred years, strikes, official or unofficial, have been a constant feature of the industrial scene. Throughout this long period, the trade unions have found no more effective weapon in disputes with employers than the concerted withdrawal of their labour. Employers and governments, on the other hand, have frequently tried every form of legal sanction to curb or prevent strikes, but without success. It seems that strikes are inevitable in an industrial society and that when official strikes are reduced in number by the introduction of complicated agreements and negotiating procedures, this process, in itself induces numerous unofficial strikes when long delays are incurred by these very procedures in settling urgent grievances.

From the Statute of Artificers in 1563 it was a criminal offence for a workman to strike in this country if he thereby broke his contract with the employer. Between 1799 and 1824 the Combination Acts were in force. During the whole of that period, all forms of working-class "combinations" or trade unions were forbidden. To strike was a criminal offence against these Acts. Only in 1824-25 were the Acts repealed and strikes legalised for a narrow range of purposes, provided they involved nothing that the courts regarded as violence or intimidation.

The next few years saw the emergence of many trade unions, some of which had existed before under the guise of Friendly Societies. Among the first were the miners, the textile workers, the building tradesmen and skilled craftsmen in a number of industries. Soon the idea of a wider and stronger union won support.

In 1830, John Doherty, the leader of the Lancashire cotton spinners, formed the National Association for the Protection of Labour. It was strongest among the cotton workers in Lancashire, but it also attracted mechanics, miners, potters and other trades in the North West and Midlands. During its two years of existence it

ix

had an organisation of 150 affiliated trades unions with a membership of between ten and twenty thousand. The main aim was to resist wage cuts. Although the National Association was short lived, the idea of the unity and solidarity of labour continued to develop. The lead was given by the Operative Builders' Union, which by 1833 had become a national organisation with forty thousand members. Its aim was "to advance and equalise the price of labour."[1]

In February, 1834, trade union delegates met and formed the Grand National Consolidated Trades Union. It was inspired by the ideals and ideas of Robert Owen and its immediate success was phenomenal. Workers joined in thousands, including agricultural labourers, women and non-manual workers. Unfortunately, Robert Owen and his followers were unable to give adequate leadership and Owen, himself, was against strikes. In spite of this, innumerable strikes broke out and the organisation was unable to cope with the situation. Eventually the focal point became Derby where 1,500 men, women and children were locked out by their employers for refusing to denounce the union.

The authorities became alarmed at this increase in trade union activity and took the offensive by arresting George and James Loveless and four other agricultural labourers in Tolpuddle, Dorset. They were accused of administering illegal oaths while forming a branch of the Friendly Society of Agricultural Labourers. After a trial at Dorchester Assizes, they were sentenced to seven years transportation. The Grand National Consolidated Trades Union organised a huge demonstration in Copenhagen Fields, London, to protest against the sentences. Robert Owen was conspicuous in leading the protest movement which ultimately secured the release of most of the prisoners.

In spite of the efforts that were put into the Grand National, it did not survive long. Before the end of a year, it had collapsed. It was too ambitious a scheme for its day. A much stronger base was needed at grass roots level before such an imposing edifice could be erected.

I

After the Reform Act of 1832 by which the bulk of the middle class was enfranchised and the workers were excluded, there was understandable disillusionment on the part of the working class. Their lack of representation inevitably led to a movement for further parliamentary reform. The first Chartist Petition with its six points was drawn up in 1838 and a movement to spread the agitation rapidly developed. The Chartist movement attracted many active workers and trade unionists and one whose ideas found ready acceptance was William Benbow. He advocated the idea of a general strike involving all workers. He wrote, printed and published his ideas in a pamphlet called "Grand National Holiday and Congress of the Productive Classes." These ideas had considerable impact on the Chartists and influenced events in 1842.

In May 1842, the second Charter petition with over three million signatures was presented and rejected. This increased the bitterness of the working class. In addition, wages were being reduced and prices were rising. There was poverty and a cholera epidemic. A storm of protest broke out over the North of England, Scotland and parts of Wales, with Lancashire as the storm centre. Towards the end of July, the workers of Ashton, Stalybridge and Hyde held a meeting at which strike action was decided upon. On 4th August, the workers in a Stalybridge mill stopped work and marched from factory to factory closing down the works by pulling out the boiler plugs. By 9th August the strike had spread and reached the Manchester area. It was estimated that no work was done in an area fifty miles around Manchester for a week. The immediate demand of the strikers was for a wage increase to restore the old rates. But on 7th August, at a huge meeting on Mottram Moor, it was decided not to return to work until the demands of the Charter were met. Delegate meetings of trade unionists in Manchester on 11th, 12th and 15th August voted overwhelmingly to continue the strike until "the People's Charter becomes the law of the land."[2]

This was probably the first occasion in history in which a strike based on economic demands had, in the course of struggle, assumed political aims. The strike was doomed to failure. Most of the delegates at the Chartist Conference were inexperienced. When they met in Manchester on 16th August they had no understanding of the strike movement and did not recognise its potential. They were not able to give the necessary leadership. Strike Committees had been set up in some localities, but they had no funds and the long crisis had depleted the finances of the workers. The manufacturers at first encouraged the workers because trade was at a low ebb, but when they saw the potential dangers of the strike, they became alarmed and allied themselves with the Government. Stern repressive measures were begun in which 1,500 workers were arrested and 54 sentenced to transportation. As so often happened, the workers lost the immediate struggle but gained immeasurably in experience.

II

As the Chartist movement declined in influence, the workers turned to trade unionism as the best means of conducting their economic struggles. The new unions were very different from the poorly organised trades associations of the early period. The unions of the new type were business-like, well organised and practical in approach. As early as 1844, the Miners' Association of Great Britain appointed a full-time solicitor, W. P. Roberts, to conduct cases in the courts. The Amalgamated Society of Engineers was formed in 1850. They had a Head Office in London and a full-time General Secretary. When the Carpenters, Iron-Founders, Bricklayers and Shoemakers also acquired Secretaries, these officials worked together in what the Webbs called, "almost . . . a Cabinet of the Trade Union movement".[3] This powerful group, they called "the Junta".

Although the "Junta" was extremely influential, it was not representative of the whole trade union movement of the time. The newly formed amalgamations which they controlled consisted of those sections of the working class who were highly skilled and

occupied a superior position in the rapidly developing class struc-
ture because of the need for ever more complex buildings and
machinery. Other sections of the workers such as the miners, textile
workers and those in iron and steel trades developed their unions
along different lines. The leaders of the new unions were mainly
in favour of social peace and a conciliatory attitude in industrial
disputes, but the rank and file were not always willing to accept
their advice and many militant struggles did take place.

One of the outstanding episodes in the 1850s was the attempt
by the London building workers to reduce the working day from
ten hours (which had been won in 1834), to nine hours. By 1857,
an agitation was started to reduce the working day. In the following
year there was a trade depression which gave rise to unemployment.
In 1859, the building trades set up a joint committee of the five
unions which was called "The Conference of the United Building
Trades". George Potter, of the Progressive Society of Carpenters
and Joiners, was the leading spirit. When negotiations with the
employers broke down in the middle of 1859, the Master Builders
were determined to break the trade union organisation and
appealed to the Government for assistance. It became clear to the
unions that the very principle of combination was being attacked
and help was sent to the building workers from many parts of the
country. The Engineers donated three thousand pounds which
certainly helped in the protracted struggle. One result of the unity
that developed during the builders' strike was the formation of the
London Trades Council.

III

Until the middle of the nineteenth century, Britain had been the
"workshop of the world" and the initiator of most technical
developments. The second half of the century saw the rest of
Europe and the United States of America catching up. In order to
compete in this growing market, Britain had to expand her productive forces even more rapidly. This gave rise to a vast army of

workers many of whom lacked the traditions and skill of their predecessors. By 1880, Britain's industrial monopoly was ended but trade unionism was still represented by such men as Henry Broadhurst and John Burnett who put their faith in the Liberal Party and the skilled craftsmen.

However, new forces were calling for a fresh approach and it was the Socialists who set the pace. Tom Mann and John Burns, both skilled engineers, recognised that the mass of unskilled workers were unorganised. They joined with Ben Tillett and Will Thorne to tackle the problem. In 1888, the Socialists led the match girls at Bryant and May's factory in the East End of London to success. The gas workers then went on strike and won an eight-hour shift instead of twelve hours and formed themselves into the Gas-workers and General Labourers' Union. In addition to the reduction in their hours they won sixpence a shift wage increase.

These victories gave the initiative to other unskilled workers. In 1889, the London dockers went on strike for four weeks and won their demand for a minimum wage of sixpence an hour. This was one of the most far-reaching struggles in the history of the trade union movement and has been immortalised as the fight for the "docker's tanner". In the following year 200,000 unskilled workers joined a trade union and the Dockers' Union spread to all the major ports.

The railwaymen, seamen, miners and agricultural workers all increased their membership and this situation reacted on the craft unions which also grew rapidly. During the period 1889-1891, over sixty new Trades Councils were formed.

This development of trade union organisation did not go un-challenged. The employers decided to sharpen their weapons. In 1897, they locked out the engineering workers for thirty weeks and then imposed harsh "terms of settlement". The employers also supported an organisation of "blacklegs" run by William Collison. This "Free Labour Association" was a band of professional strike breakers who were transported to any part of the country where trades unionists were on strike. They received the full support of the police, press and armed forces. In two of the biggest miners' strikes, that of 1893 and the South Wales Strike of 1898, troops were called out at the request of the coalowners and striking miners were fired on. At Featherstone, in Yorkshire, several miners were killed.

Towards the end of the century, working-class opinion became convinced that the Liberal Party was not the vehicle of emancipation that had been hoped. The Labour Party was formed and in the General Election of 1906, gained twenty nine seats in Parliament. The political wing of the labour movement was largely Fabian in tendency but the industrial workers were in no mood for gradualism. Real wages fell considerably during the period 1911-1914. The elected representatives in Parliament failed to show any convincing opposition. A need arose for a clearly defined working-class leadership and this was supplied by the Syndicalists.

Syndicalism had its origin in France and had spread to the United States. It advocated the complete supremacy of the trade unions and maintained that the producers should obtain control of all industries and all services through a series of strikes which were to culminate in a general strike to take over national control. In the autumn of 1910, two hundred Syndicalists met in Manchester and formed "The Industrial Syndicalist Education League". Tom Mann was the leading influence in this organisation.

He said that

"economic emancipation of the working class can only be secured by the working class asserting its power in workshops, factories, warehouses, mills and mines, on ships and boats and engines, and wherever work is performed, ever extending their control over the tools of production until, by the power of the organised proletariat, capitalist production shall entirely cease and the industrial socialist republic shall be ushered in, and thus the Socialist Revolution realised."[4]

Events during the period 1911-1914 show the organising power and influence of the Syndicalists. The pattern of strikes in one industry after another was planned to end in a general strike in 1914 which might well have succeeded had it not been for the outbreak of the first World War. The influence of the Syndicalists far outweighed their numbers.

The "Great Unrest" as it became called, was a continuation of the upsurge of the unskilled labourers begun in 1889. The dockers were again in the forefront with the transport workers, miners and railwaymen following closely. The transport unions gained nearly half a million new members in these years and the Workers Union which had 5,000 members in 111 branches in 1910 had expanded to 91,000 members in 567 branches by 1913. There was also an advance in women's trade union activity. The National Federation of Women Workers was formed to cater for women in unorganised trades. Women played a notable part in the strikes that took place. A high point was reached in Bermondsey in 1911 when some 24 separate factories struck, and, after three weeks, wage advances were won in eighteen of them.

The strikes that took place in the 1911 period among the transport workers were sparked off by the seamen. They went on strike in June, 1910. The dockers, the railway porters and the carters all refused to handle cargoes. Immediately following the seamen's strike, the dockers came out and the seamen stopped work again in sympathy. During the month of July, 1911, one trade after another followed the lead of the shipping workers. From the brewery workers who decided to brew only "union" ale to the girls at the Walton rubber works who objected to the unfair system of fines, the unrest escalated. Just as the shipowners and dockers were near agreement, the railway workers began what was to prove the most bitter phase of the summer's struggles.

Leaders of the railwaymen refused to support the strike, so Tom Mann accepted the leadership and headed a Joint Strike Committee which took over the organisation. In Liverpool, a pregnant situation arose which was quickly recognised by the Liberal Government. The Joint Strike Committee virtually took over the organisation of the City. No essential services were carried out unless authorised by the Committee. Post was delivered only by courtesy of the Committee. The Government acted swiftly to prevent the maturation of such a potentially dangerous situation and by the end of August, 1911 the railwaymen were back at work with their demands largely met.

The railwaymen were followed by the miners. After opening skirmishes, the miners finally struck on 1st March, 1912. A million miners ceased work as one man. Although the demand for a national minimum rate was not met, the Government displayed exceptional haste in drafting a Minimum Wage Bill which they managed to pass by the end of March. This set out machinery for the determination of district minimum wages.

The transport workers, the railwaymen and the miners were the big guns in the "Great Unrest". The year 1913 showed a proliferation of disputes in many other branches of industry. While the number of strikes in 1911 was 872 and in 1912 it was 834, by 1913 it had risen to 1,459. On the other hand the numbers of workers involved dropped from 1,462,000 in 1912 to 664,000 in 1913.

The Irish workers also took part in the struggle. At the beginning of 1913, the Dublin port workers went on strike. The employers refused to take on any worker if he was a member of a union. As week succeeded week, the number of strikers increased, many workers and their families nearing the point of starvation. The English trade union movement together with the Co-operative Societies showed them that an injury to one is an injury to all. Food parcels were sent in specially chartered ships. The Co-operative Wholesale Society supplied the contents and the money to pay for them was collected in factories and mines all over Britain. The eight months' strike was indecisive, but the wholehearted support of the English labour movement prevented a major defeat for the Irish workers.

The cost of living continued to rise. Trade Union organisation continued to develop. Everything in 1914 pointed to a culmination of the activity in a general stoppage of all workers. Lord Askwith said at the time that, "within a comparatively short time there may be movements in this country coming to a head of which recent events have been a small foreshadowing."[5] At the beginning of August, 1914 there were 100 strikes in progress. At the end of the month there were only twenty. The war with Germany had begun.

After the outbreak of war there was considerable dislocation of industry, long hours of work and constant demands by the employers to abandon established workshop practices. The trade union leaders decided on a policy of industrial truce and made their peace with the Government. After a Conference between the Government and the trade unions at the Treasury, the Munitions of War Acts (1915-1917) were passed. These abolished the right to strike for the duration of the war, suspended trade union rules, introduced dilution (allowing unskilled labour to do skilled work) and by the use of "leaving certificates", prevented men from changing their jobs.

This industrial conscription did not, however, prevent strikes from breaking out. From July, 1915, to July, 1916, there were 350,000 workers from the Clyde, Lancashire, Sheffield, Coventry and South Wales involved in strikes. In spite of the provisions of the Acts, action was only taken against 1,612 of them. The Minister of Munitions, Mr. Lloyd George, was so anxious to avoid trouble that he went to the South Wales coalfield himself and conceded the men's claim rather than take it through the Courts.

In this situation where the trade union leaders became, as the Webbs said, "part of the social machinery of the state"[6], new leaders emerged. The Clyde Workers Committee was the model for similar committees in other industrial centres. In 1916, The National Shop Stewards and Workers Committee Movement was formed. The unit of organisation was the Works Committee in each factory. Representative shop stewards were elected in each department and this committee sent representatives to a District Committee. The National Administrative Council consisted of delegates from the District Committees. However, in spite of the representative character of the National Council, it had no executive power and all policy matters had to be referred back to the rank and file. This was a natural reaction against officials engendered by what was regarded as the betrayal by the trade union leaders, but in effect it was ponderous and prevented the Movement from giving convincing leadership.

When the slump came in 1921, the Shop Stewards Movement declined and many stewards were victimised. However, the integration of the Shop Stewards into the trade union machinery considerably strengthened the whole movement.

The end of the war ushered in an era of apparent prosperity. Prices rose sharply, but wages also rose. The growing realisation of the importance of the Russian Revolution of 1917, sent the returning workers into the trade unions, political parties and the co-operative movement. The workers in this period were on the offensive. In the General Election of 1918, the Labour Party became, for the first time, a national electoral force. Although they gained only sixty-one seats, the defeat of the Independent Liberals gave them the status of an official opposition.

The year of 1919 was critical. The miners determined to strike in support of their demand for nationalisation of the industry. In January, they decided to press their claims in conjunction with the railwaymen and the transport workers. They called themselves the "Triple Alliance". They were deflected from their purpose by the promise of a Royal Commission under Sir John Sankey to report on the coal industry. Further threatened strikes were forestalled by the setting up of a National Industrial Conference to consider hours of work, a minimum wage and the establishment of a joint standing National Industrial Council. The protracted negotiations of this Commission and the promising report when it was published did succeed in preventing serious unrest for a time. The Sankey Commission issued an interim report in March, 1919, and by the reduction of the underground shift to seven hours and the increase of wages by two shillings a shift, the miners were induced to withdraw the strike notices. The Commission also recommended nationalisation of the industry with some workers' control. The disillusion which followed in the mining industry when it was realised that the Government had no intention of implementing these suggestions, acted as a goad to the miners and was a contributory factor leading to the General Strike in 1926.

In the summer of 1919, 300,000 cotton workers in Lancashire struck for a 30% increase in wages and a forty-eight hour week.

There were also threatened strikes in the Police and the armed forces. Demobilisation was not proceeding fast enough and in some camps mutinies were narrowly averted by a relaxation of discipline. In 1918, there were 1,165 strikes involving 1,116,000 workers, but in 1919, while the number of strikes was similar (1,352), the numbers involved had risen to 2,519,000 — more than in the peak year of the Great Unrest, 1912.

At the time of these industrial struggles, considerable reorganisation was taking place in the Labour Movement. Small unions were merging to form the large amalgamations that we know today. The Amalgamated Engineering Union, The Transport and General Workers' Union and the National Union of General and Municipal Workers were all developed in the immediate post-war years and were to dominate the Labour Party Conferences and the Trades Union Congress with their block votes from that time. The Amalgamated Union of Building Trades Workers and the Amalgamated Society of Woodworkers were also formed in 1919.

The apparent post-war prosperity soon showed itself to be an illusion. In 1921, there was a slump and considerable unemployment. The miners were the first to be attacked. In March of that year, the coal owners locked out the workers after their demand for a considerable cut in wages had been firmly rejected. The miners invoked the aid of the Triple Alliance and a strike of railway and transport workers was called for 12th April. The rank and file were enthusiastic. The officials were less so. On the day that the sympathetic strike was due to begin, the miners and the Government went into conference and the strike was postponed to 15th April, a Friday. Frank Hodges, Secretary of the Miners' Federation, made a statement to Members of Parliament which was later repudiated by his Executive Committee. On the pretext that the miners had rejected the possibility of a settlement, the transport and railway union leaders called off the strike. Eventually, the miners had to return to work defeated. This Friday became known in trade union history as "Black Friday".

During the years immediately preceding the General Strike, unemployment became widespread and industrial disputes increased. Cuts in wages and increased hours of work led to further disillusion. The Labour Party increased its number of M.P.s by nearly eighty in the 1922 election and added another forty-eight in 1924. The Liberals joined forces with Labour to push out the Conservatives and the first Labour Government was formed with Ramsay MacDonald as Prime Minister. A strike wave was mounting as the new Government took office. The number of recorded strikes rose from 628 in 1923 to 710 in 1924. The numbers involved rose from 405,000 to 613,000. This restiveness increased when the Labour Government was defeated at an election in the November after it took office.

The two years leading up to the General Strike were difficult ones for the British labour movement. The miners were heading for a showdown. The rest of the trade unions were preparing to support them. If it could hardly be called the lull before the storm, it could certainly be characterised as a period of tightening belts and preparation for battle.

V

It was not accidental that the General Strike arose from the issue of miners' wages. The miners had been in the vanguard both in 1921 and 1925. The wages question was the kernel of the situation and it united the whole trade union movement. The coal industry in 1925 was in a state of crisis and the coalowners could offer only one solution, to reduce wages.

The Conservative Government made its intentions quite clear. The Prime Minister, Mr. Stanley Baldwin, told the miners that not only must they accept a reduction in wages, but all workers in the country would have to accept reduced wages to help put industry on its feet. Intensive and elaborate preparations were made by the Government. A strike breaking system which had been set up in 1923 was now revived and extended. It was called the "Organisation for the Maintenance of Supplies". The country was divided into districts with a staff of military officers in charge of transport and supplies. Stocks of coal were built up and a secret circular was issued to all Local Authorities outlining a scheme of control applicable in the event of a strike. Preparations were also made to assemble troops and to concentrate the Fleet on the industrial ports. Auxiliary transport was organised, and with the help of private cars, a fleet of 200,000 vehicles was registered for use. An inner Cabinet of Baldwin, Churchill, Birkenhead and Joynson-Hicks was appointed to take over in case of emergency.

In the face of these extraordinary preparations, the trade union leaders took no positive steps. The trade union movement remained totally unprepared to deal with the situation. Walter Citrine said in 1927:

"So far as preparations for a general strike was concerned the General Council never attempted to do such a thing, and in my opinion they would have failed most lamentably if they had attempted anything of the kind."[7]

When the report of the Samuel Commission, which had been set up to inquire into the mining industry, was published, it contained proposals for wage cuts and longer hours of work for the miners. The coalowners naturally seized the opportunity and posted notices demanding wage reductions, an increase in hours and district agreements. The General Council of the Trades Union Congress then called a Conference of Union Executives which voted by 3,653,527 to 49,911 in favour of strike action in support of the miners.

On 3rd May, 1926, printers working on the *Daily Mail* refused to print an article written by the editor, Thomas Marlowe, headed "FOR KING AND COUNTRY" which they regarded as a vicious attack on the working class. The printers decided that the paper would only be produced if the offending article were withdrawn. It was not and that night the *Daily Mail* was not printed. The Government reacted immediately and demanded that the General Strike be called off unconditionally. The following day, 4th May, the strike began.

The Government recognised from the outset the political character of the strike. Their chief spokesman was Winston Churchill who edited the daily news sheet *The British Gazette* from the Morning

Post press. He assiduously cultivated the picture of the Government as the upholder of democracy and the freedom of the press. Baldwin, on 5th May, wrote, "The General Strike is a challenge to Parliament. It is the road to anarchy and ruin."[8]

The General Council, on the other hand, published the *British Worker*, which went on the defensive from the start, emphasising that the strike was not a challenge to the Government. While the leaders displayed every sign of weakness, the workers responded enthusiastically to the call to cease work. Mass pickets, thousands strong, stopped all transport in the big cities except that marked "By permission of the T.U.C.". Trades Councils, Councils of Action and Strike Committees led the struggle.

London was like an armed camp and there were troops in Hull and Marines in Middlesbrough. Troops and armoured cars escorted food convoys with orders to get through at all costs.

Some seven thousand workers were arrested and many convicted and sent to gaol: mostly for "intimidation", "obstruction" or breaches of the regulations made by the Government under the Emergency Powers Act 1920. Mr. Justice Astbury in an important judgement declared the strike altogether illegal: and was echoed within a few hours by Sir John Simon in the House of Commons. Though bad law this was effective propaganda, and the trade union leaders saw that their own turn might soon come. This was one factor which led to the strike being called off without any solution to the problem of the miners' wages.

The decision to call off the strike was received with dismay and anger by the rank and file. The return to work was spasmodic. Local employers tried to impose their own harsh terms on the strikers and a stubborn fight had to be waged to prevent the workers from being completely crushed. Almost a week passed before there was a general resumption of work and the miners were left alone to fight for a further seven months before they returned to the pits defeated.

The Conservative Government moreover took advantage of the defeat of the unions by passing the Trade Disputes and Trade Unions Act of 1927 which pronounced the General Strike illegal as well as any sympathetic strikes which were held by the courts to be designed to coerce the Government or inflict hardship on the community. Picketing was restricted. Civil Servants were banned from belonging to any association not consisting wholly of state employees, and trade unions could collect political funds only from those members who had actually signed a form expressing their desire to contribute. In many important respects the unions were back to the 1850s.

The early thirties were characterised by severe unemployment and hardship. The militant struggles of the Lancashire weavers against wage cuts and the "more-looms" system and the refusal of the London busmen to accept the wage cut that their union leaders were prepared to accept, relieved the general gloom of the industrial scene. Many workers were without the chance of a wage at all and the huge demonstrations of the unemployed testified to the desperate situation.

Towards the end of the thirties, rearmament introduced a "boom" period. The passivity of the official trade union machinery inevitably resulted in numerous unofficial strikes. Many of these strikes were for trade union recognition and the establishment of shop stewards. The developing aircraft industry was particularly active. The outbreak of war in 1939, although it ended an epoch of industrial action possibly unsurpassed since Chartist days, also ended a period of comparative industrial stagnation. The trade union movement did not really recover from the effects of the 1926 defeat until the war ended.

VI

When the period of the "phoney war" was at an end, the trade union movement gave its support to the war effort. Joint Production Committees were set up at factory and district levels in the engineering industry. These played a significant part in furthering war production.

The Conditions of Employment and National Arbitration Order (S.R. & O. 1940, No. 1305) was in force from 1940 until 1951.

This was similar to the Munitions of War Act, 1915, which made arbitration compulsory and strikes illegal. Between the date of its introduction in 1940 and January 1944, there were 5,000 prosecutions arising out of strikes which involved one and a half million workers. But only 2,000 of these were convicted. The first large-scale prosecution under the Order was in January 1942, when 1,050 miners at Betteshanger Colliery in Kent were summonsed. Three of the leaders were put in prison and the rest were fined. In spite of this, the men refused to return to work until a satisfactory offer was made to them five days later. Only nine of the men who were fined actually paid. Warrants were taken out against the rest, but they were not executed. In 1944 there was a confusing wage award made to the miners. This gave rise to widespread strikes in most of the major coalfields. Although there were 821,000 strikers (or possibly, *because* there were so many) there were only three prosecutions. If sufficiently large numbers of people disregard the law, it seems it loses its efficacy.

The trade union movement emerged from the war considerably strengthened. Through the decisive part that Labour had played in the war against Fascism, it had reached full maturity and its voice was heard in all the affairs of the nation. At the 1945 General Election the Labour Party was returned to power with an overall majority. This was the first time so clear a mandate had been given to Labour.

The trade unions also gained in strength. Membership of those unions affiliated to the T.U.C. rose from 4,669,186 in 1939 to 6,575,654 in 1945. By 1969 it had risen again to 8,875,381.

VII

Throughout the post-war period the constant cry of politicians of both parties, as well as that of the employers, was that the country was undergoing economic crises due to excessive wage demands. As early as 1947, Sir Stafford Cripps, the Labour Chancellor of the Exchequer, and Mr. Attlee, the Prime Minister, called for wage restraint. In 1949, the pound was devalued and the unions were again exhorted to exercise restraint in pursuance of their wage claims. The General Council of the T.U.C. accepted the policy at first, but at the Trades Union Congress in September, 1949, it was rejected.

The Conservative Governments in 1951 and 1952 tried, without success, to convince the trade union leaders of the validity of restraint in their applications for more money. It was not easy to make a case for wage restraint when prices continued to rise and profits showed no signs of arresting their upward trend. During the period 1955-1957 there was a further crisis and another attempt was made to curb wage claims, but the Trades Union Congress made its position quite clear. It re-iterated that "Congress asserts the right of Labour to bargain on equal terms with Capital."[9]

The crisis recurred in 1961 and again in 1964. In each case the workers were called on to accept virtual cuts in their standard of living. In an effort to co-operate with the Labour Government, the T.U.C. General Council signed the "Joint Statement of Intent on Productivity, Prices and Incomes".

By February, 1966, it had become clear that the Joint Statement was wishful thinking and it was replaced by the Prices and Incomes Act, 1966. This provided for a four months' moratorium on wage increases with legal sanctions to enforce it. Penalties for striking, whether officially or unofficially, in support of a wage claim which had been referred to the Board and not approved were put at a maximum of £100 on summary conviction and £500 on indictment.

VIII

In the two centuries of trade union history, employers and governments have co-operated on numerous occasions to curb and stultify the unions by legal action. The Combination Acts of 1799 and 1800 were one of the first serious attempts to prevent workers using their collective strength to raise their standard of living. A Sheffield employer put the case clearly when he said "the law is harsh, for wages are difficult to be advanced except by combination"[10] Gravener Henson, one of the most prominent trade union leaders of the time, expressed similar views in his evidence to a select committee in 1824:

"I have always considered that the Combination Laws had the effect of lowering the rate of wages; but the men in our county have considered them so oppressive, their motto has been, 'If you will find gaols, we will find bodies'."

The workers struggled at that time to achieve the repeal of the Acts. But although only limited rights were won when the Acts were repealed in 1824, the legalisation of unions marked an important victory.

In the year that the Labour Party was formed, there was another attack on trade union activity. In 1900, there was a strike of Taff Vale railwaymen. The Railway Company obtained damages and costs amounting to £23,000. Altogether the case cost the Society £43,000. This meant in effect that a trade union could be held answerable in damages for any tortious acts of its officials both local and national. N. A. Citrine said that the Taff Vale decision was:

"a smashing blow to trade union activity. Having developed doctrines that made most union activity unlawful, the courts now made the unions liable to respond in damages for any act that might fall within the condemnation of those doctrines"[12]

Clearly this was an attack on the right to strike as well as the right to organise. The labour movement rallied to the defence of the unions and in the campaign that developed, the Labour Party grew and flourished. The Act that was passed in 1906, the Trade Disputes Act, became the charter of the unions. It specifically provided that no civil action could be taken against a trade union in respect of any tortious act committed by or on behalf of the union. The Act also provided a statutory right of peaceful picketing; and protection from actions for damages against union officials (or anyone else) for conspiracy or for inducing breaches of contract, so long as they acted 'in contemplation or furtherance of a trade dispute' — i.e. broadly, in a strike situation. Many of these gains were, of course, destroyed by the punitive measures of the Trade

Disputes Act 1927 after the General Strike, but were restored by the post-war Labour Government which repealed the 1927 Act in 1946.

It is, therefore, ironical that the first serious post-war attempt to weaken the unions' position was inaugurated by a Labour Government. Mr. Harold Wilson and Mrs. Barbara Castle opened the door to the Conservatives' Industrial Relations Bill by introducing the White Paper, *In Place of Strife*. The main object of this document was to put such difficulties in the way of strikes that they would cease to be an effective weapon in the trade union armoury.

The trade union movement saw the dangers in the White Paper and acted to compel the government to withdraw the Bill based upon it. Their efforts however were frustrated for, when the Conservatives were returned to power in the election of June 1970, they were able to put their own plans into effect all the more easily because of the deep divisions in the Labour movement which the previous Bill had engendered.

Their first major piece of legislation was their own Industrial Relations Bill, which contained much more severe measures against the unions and was bitterly opposed by them. This Bill has now been passed as the Industrial Relations Act 1971; It repeals the whole of the 1906 Act, while re-enacting some of its protective clauses. Others, however, now apply only to *official* strikes of *registered* trade unions: and beside the ordinary civil liability in tort, there is an elaborate catalogue of "unfair industrial practices" which are likely, in practice, to affect almost any major strike and the great majority of small ones. For these both individuals and unions can be made to pay "compensation" to employers or non-unionists — which though not ·called a fine or damages, will feel very much the same when it is inflicted. Whether the new Act will do anything to solve the problem of strikes; or whether it will share the fate of its predecessors — we shall see in the course of time.

Notes

[1] R. W. Postgate, *The Builders' History*, page 68 (1923).
[2] Feargus O'Connor, *The Trial of F. O'Connor and Fifty Eight Others*, page 49 (1843).
[3] Sidney and Beatrice Webb, *The History of Trade Unionism 1666-1920*, page 233 (1920).
[4] Tom Mann, A Two Fold Warning, *The Industrial Syndicalist* (April 1911).
[5] Lord Askwith, *Industrial Problems and Disputes*, page 849 (1920).
[6] Sidney and Beatrice Webb, *op. cit.*, page 635.
[7] Trades Union Congress General Council, *National Strike Special Conference Report*, page 42 (1927).
[8] *British Gazette, 5th May, 1926.*
[9] Trades Union Congress, *Report, 1956*, page 528.
[10] T. A. Ward, *Peeps Into The Past*, page 216 (1909).
[11] Select Committee on Artizans and Machinery, Fourth Report, page 271 (1824).
[12] Norman Arthur Citrine, *Trade Union Law*, page 16 (3rd edn. 1967).

ACKNOWLEDGEMENTS

We are very much indebted to Mr. John B. Smethurst for permission to use some of the material contained in his lecture "Ballads of the coal-fields". We wish to thank Messrs. George Allen & Unwin Ltd. (ARNOT, R. P., *The Miners: Years of Struggle;* KENNEY, R., *Men and Rails*); The Bodley Head (MURPHY, J. T., *New Horizons*); Hutchinson Publishing Group Ltd. (MACREADY, Sir Nevil, *Annals of an active life*); Lawrence & Wishart, Ltd. (BELL, T., *Pioneering Days;* GALLACHER, W., *Revolt on the Clyde*); and Weidenfeld & Nicholson, Ltd. (REYNOLDS & JUDGE, *The Night the police went on strike),* for permission to use copyright material.

The passages included in this volume are taken from many sources. A large number have been quoted from books and pamphlets in the substantial collection of trade union historical material in the possession of Ruth and Edmund Frow in Manchester. Wherever possible the source of quoted material is given. If inadvertently we have omitted to acknowledge or seek permission to use material still in copyright, this will have been due entirely to our inability to trace the authors or publishers and we would be grateful to have these brought to our attention so that we can make the necessary amends.

Finally, we wish to thank Mr. Geoffrey de N. Clark for helpful advice and encouragement and Messrs. Charles Knight & Co. Ltd. for their constant helpfulness well beyond the call of duty.

R. & E.F.
M.K.

1. The First Union-Organised Strike

[*BEFORE the industrial revolution, hours of labour, rates of wages, conditions of apprentices and methods of work were laid down by a series of statutes and ordinances, mostly originating in the trade and craft guilds of the middle ages and subsequently embodied in Statute Law.*

Many early trade unions were formed to counter the non-observance by the employers of these statutory regulations affecting labour. The unions endeavoured to enforce the laws, while the employers, in many cases, sought to evade them. These were the circumstances in which the first notable union-organised strike took place.]

THE REVOLT OF THE WEAVERS, 1756

". . . Woollen manufactures was one of the oldest staple industries of the kingdom. The Trade Guilds and Craft Guilds of the Woollen Weavers were among the earlier of those established, and were of great importance. The trade was subsequently regulated by 5 and 6 Edward VI., c. 22; by 2 and 8 Mary, c. 11, as to the number of looms one weaver might have; and generally as to apprentices, &c., by 5 Elizabeth, c. 4. The regulations as to the assessment of wages by the justices appears to have fallen into disuse – by reason, perhaps, of the strong combinations of the weavers, those being sufficient to ensure sufficient wages, for a long period prior to 1720. In that year, however, the justices were induced to fix the rate of wages, but the masters resisted the rates so fixed, and they were not enforced by law. In consequence of this, the workmen strengthened their combinations. The masters then determined to attack the right of association. Accordingly, in 1725, combinations of workmen employed in the wollen manufacturers were prohibited by 12 George II., c. 34.

The workmen were thus left in the unfortunate position of having no fixed legal rate of wages, and no right of association to

1

enforce a rate, based upon the principle of supply and demand. The injustice of the situation was recognised, and in the following year, 1726, an Act (13 Geo. I., c. 23) was passed ordering the justices once more to fix the rate of wages in the woollen trades. Again the statutory enactment seems to have become inoperative, for we find little reference to it until the year 1756, when the workmen petitioned the justices to fix such rate of wages, according to the law; but as the masters presented a counter petition the justices refused. Here, again, the men were left without a remedy; they were prohibited from combining, and the justices refused to carry out the provisions of the statute as regards rates of wages. This state of things becoming unbearable the weavers revolted; they struck work, and drove the journeymen who continued working from their looms. This strike led to serious riots, and resulted in a loss to the country, estimated from £15,000 to £20,000, but it was so far successful that the masters gave way. Having agreed to certain proposals of the workmen, peace was restored. The justices were thereupon ordered, by 29 Geo. III., c. 33, to settle the rate of wages in the woollen trades yearly."

GEORGE HOWELL, Great Strikes: Their Origin,
Cost and Results (*C.W.S. Annual 1889*)

2. Trade Unions Illegal, 1799-1824

[IN 1799 and 1800 the Combination Acts made both trade unions and strikes illegal and empowered a single justice of the peace to sentence summarily a trade unionist to two months imprisonment. Longer terms could be inflicted on indictment, and this was frequently done. These Acts were in force until 1824, but despite the ease of prosecution, strikes were frequent. Moreover, since the unions were driven underground, industrial action took more violent forms, including the destruction of machinery, the burning of agricultural and industrial premises, and occasionally violence to persons.]

BITTER DISPUTES

". . . No "great strike" was really possible during the existence of the Combination Laws; but many of the labour disputes in that period were very bitter, and some were conducted with personal violence, with gross outrages, and with reckless destruction of property. It is, however, perfectly certain that, in most cases where violence occurred, the masters acted with so high a hand, that even the excesses of the workmen are to be excused — were even excused by the report of the Committee which sat in 1824. The Combination Laws were so cruel and tyrannical that they were condemned by the Legislature, and were repealed. Among the strikes which took place prior to 1824, of which any authentic record exists, . . . the following may be mentioned: — In 1810 there was a strike of carpenters in London for an advance of 4s. per week; after lasting five weeks, the men were successful. In 1816 the masters determined to reduce their wages by 3s. per week; after a resistance of fourteen weeks the men had to give in; but in 1818 they regained 2s. per week without a formal strike. In 1812 the cotton weavers of Glasgow struck; the strike lasted six weeks; no fewer than 40,000

3

looms were stopped by this strike. The leaders were prosecuted and imprisoned; the association was broken up, and the men gave in. In 1810 the cotton spinners struck work; the masters closed their mills, and compelled all their workpeople to abandon the union before resuming work. The Dewsbury strike, in 1821, lasted till 1823 – only one mill being called out at a time. This plan proved successful. The strike of the ship-sawyers of Liverpool, in 1816, for higher wages, lasted fourteen weeks, when they had to submit to a reduction instead. This reduction in wages lasted until 1823, when the men again struck. The masters employed a larger number of apprentices, and also imported sawyers from other districts, during the strike. Some of the latter were violently ill used, one being murdered; one of the three men implicated was hanged for the murder, at Lancaster. One of the master's yards was also set on fire. Several other acts of violence seem to have been committed by the sawyers.

The action of the stocking-makers of Leicester was somewhat singular. In 1813 they had a strike, which was unsuccessful, several of the men being imprisoned. The union being broken up, the wages were so reduced that the masters, in 1817, instigated the men to combine. Both parties met, and agreed upon a list of prices. But one after another the masters again began to reduce wages, so that, in 1819, the men struck, to the number of 14,000. After nine weeks' resistance the masters gave in, and agreed to abide by the statement of prices mutually fixed in 1817. In this case the public were on the side of the men, whose wages only averaged from 5s. to 7s. per week. The Lord Lieutenant of the County and the county members subscribed to the funds for keeping those on strike. Sermons were preached in the churches on their behalf, and a benefit was given in the theatre in support of the movement. The conduct of the men was most exemplary throughout. In 1821 there was a similar strike at Nottingham, lasting six weeks, a prosecution being the result, but the conviction was quashed. Where no association existed, frame breaking took place; but, apparently, not otherwise. At Howick, in 1819, the master stocking-makers attempted a reduction; the men appealed to the justices to fix the wages, as they were empowered to do. The justices admitted that they had

4

power, but refused to use it. The men then prosecuted the masters for combining to reduce their wages; the sheriff declared that the men had substantiated their charges, but no conviction followed. In 1821 the masters again attempted a further reduction; the men struck, and they remained out for 28 weeks; the masters then prosecuted 20 of the men, but the sheriff discharged them upon learning from the chief magistrate and others that the men had been perfectly peaceable all the time.

In 1810 there was an obstinate strike of colliers at the Newcastle collieries. Much violence ensued; the military were called out, and one soldier was stabbed. The strike was conducted by a "secret committee," but after lasting four weeks, the men gave in. There were also strikes amongst the coopers of London, in 1808, 1813, 1816, and 1825. For a long time their wages were regulated by the price of bread, but the men resolved to reject that standard, and succeeded. Their wages were advanced in 1813, and again in 1816, when a list was agreed upon, which lasted until 1825, at which date a new "statement" was demanded. Strikes also took place among the paper makers in Kent — the Combination Laws not being enforced, and it is said their existence even was unknown. The men, women, and children were regularly supported during a strike from the club funds.

Strikes occurred in connection with the cloth trade at Wakefield, in 1822, and again in 1824, for an advance of wages. Those who took the place of the men on strike were threatened, but no actual violence was resorted to, except the breaking of some windows and injury to a garden. In 1824 the Yorkshire weavers struck for an advance of wages, and succeeded; one employer had to pay a fine of £100 to the union, as compensation for the loss of time occasioned by the strike. Other strikes occurred in connection with this trade, the masters endeavouring to carry on with non-union men, but they were compelled to give in. The flannel weavers at Rochdale struck in 1823 and 1824 against an infringement of the wages statement of 1815; but as many of the manufacturers supported the men, the others gave in. No violence appears to have taken place during the dispute.

Several strikes occurred among the Scottish colliers, both for an advance of wages and for a rectification of the mode of measurement then adopted as to the output of coal. There does not appear to have been any violence or intimidation. The weavers, calico printers, and cotton weavers in Renfrewshire and Lanarkshire had several strikes between 1810 and 1824, and several acts of violence and some outrages occurred. In Ireland, also, especially in Dublin and Belfast, some strikes took place, chiefly in connection with the woollen and linen trades, and also among the carpenters and cabinetmakers. From 1815 to 1824 the seamen of the northern ports of England struck for advances of wages, and as to the number of hands to man the ships. Acts of violence were common, but no serious outrage occurred; in one case, however, on the Tyne, ten sail of the King's ships, 500 marines, and four regiments were sent to quell the disturbances, and some men were prosecuted . . ."

GEORGE HOWELL (*Ibid.*)

3. The Blackfaces of 1812

"IN JULY, 1812, the monthly average price of wheat was 144s. 6d. per quarter, and by that time a Secret Committee of the House of Commons had been appointed to examine the contents of "a sealed bag," containing ample materials for producing a panic. The report of the Commons was in substance − "That alarming disturbances, destructive to property, had prevailed in Lancashire, Yorkshire, Cheshire, Derbyshire, Nottinghamshire, and Leicestershire; that the rioters assembled in the night-time *with their faces blackened,* armed with the implements of their trades, and other offensive instruments, with which they destroyed the property of those who were obnoxious to them. They also took an oath that, while they existed under the canopy of Heaven, they would not reveal anything connected with the disturbances, under the penalty of being put out of existence by the first brother whom they should meet. It was held out to them that they might expect to be joined by other discontented persons from London, and that there were persons in the higher ranks who would also lend them support." The report of the Lords was much fuller than that of the Commons. It spoke of extensive preparations for a rebellion. "In the middle of April, a meeting was held for the purpose of being trained for military exercise. Houses were plundered by persons in disguise, and contributions were levied in the neighbourhood of Manchester, at the houses of gentlemen and farmers. A singular arrival also happened at Manchester. On the 26th and 27th of April, the people were alarmed by the appearance of some thousands of strangers in their town. The greater part of them, however, disappeared on the 28th. Part of the Local Militia had been then called out and a large military force had arrived, which, it was supposed, had overawed those who were disposed to disturbance. An apprehension, however, prevailed of a more general rising in May." Their lordships, in speaking of the cause of these disturbances, seemed bent on making them out to be quite unconnected with the

7

state of trade. The riots at Manchester were, in reality, nothing else than "meal mobs;" but this was not sufficiently alarming for their lordships, who alluded to this circumstance in a tone of determined incredulity. "The general *pretence*," say they, "was the high price of provisions." Had their report been dictated by honesty, the high price of provisions would not have been spoken of as a mere pretence. The following were the monthly averages of wheat from January to August, 1812:—

	Per quarter.			Per quarter.	
	s.	d.		s.	d.
January	105	9	May	132	6
February	105	2	June	133	10
March	112	5	July	144	6
April	125	5	August	152	3

But their lordships could see nothing but revolution in the proceedings of the rioters. "The views," it was further stated, "of some of the persons engaged have extended to revolutionary measures, of the most violent description. Their proceedings manifest a degree of caution and organization which appears to flow from the direction of some persons under whose influence they act. The general persuasion of the persons engaged in these transactions appears to be, that all the societies in the country are directed in their motions by a secret committee, and that this secret committee is therefore the great mover of the whole machine; and it is established, by the various information to which the committee has before alluded, that societies are formed in different parts of the country; that these societies are governed by their respective secret committees; for the purpose of concerting their plans; and that secret signs are arranged, by which the persons engaged in these conspiracies are known to each other . . ."

The Blackfaces of 1812. (Bolton 1839)

8

4. Cotton Strike in Scotland, 1812

[IN THE first decade of the 19th Century, weavers all over Britain were endeavouring to obtain a Minimum Wage Bill. Parliament rejected this in 1808, and despite the Combination Acts, there were great strikes of both cotton and woollen weavers in Lancashire. These gained a temporary victory but wages were soon again reduced. In 1812 there was a general strike of weavers in Scotland, lasting at least three weeks. It ended with the arrest of the Strike Committee who were sentenced to periods of imprisonment from 4 to 18 months.]

"Deputies were immediately sent to inform the country districts, that it was the opinion of the committee that no work should be done, unless the price was paid, and at a meeting of delegates from nearly eighty towns and villages, held on the 18th (Nov. 1812), in presence of the procurator fiscal of the county, (who had been invited to attend.) they declared that it was the unanimous resolution of the whole body, whom they represented, not to work under the rates declared reasonable by law. On that day 20,000 looms stopped work, and, in a few days more, they were increased to near double the number; scarcely the sound of a shuttle being heard from Aberdeen to Carlisle, connected with the cotton manufacture. Every thing remained in the most profound peace; no tumult or disturbance of any kind took place, and, excepting that greater numbers were passing to and from Glasgow, it exhibited the appearance of one continued Sunday, which in Scotland, is remarkable for its stillness and placidity.

The trade in England and Ireland had been apprized of what was intended, but no pecuniary assistance was either expected or received from them, nor could any fund be previously raised, that could have any influence on the subsistence of such a large body, which, including all the branches of the trade, involved not less than 200,000 persons. Every disposition was, however, shown to assist one another; the funds of friendly societies were borrowed, and joint securities given, for credits, in many various ways; but it was the impression we calculated on being able to make on opinion, not on pecuniary resources, or physical power, to which we looked for success. Things went on, with little variation, for more than three weeks; a few fabrics were given out, at the prices affixed by the table, but no disposition had been shown to effect any general compromise, and we soon learnt the cause. All the disposable troops in Scotland were ordered to the western counties, and cantoned in the various towns and villages; and it was rumoured, that the operatives were to be put down by force . . . The situation of the committee became most arduous and difficult, many of the operatives foreseeing what was approaching, conceived themselves treated with flagrant injustice, to be thus crushed by the mere influence of force, and disappointed, irritated, and nearly actuated by despair, were for having recourse to stronger measures, and with difficulty could be restrained from violence. We were accused by many for the paucity of our proceedings and want of energy, in not calling into action the whole body in England and Ireland, to obtain, by force, what the law had declared we were entitled to. Meetings of delegates continued to be held privately: these we still attended . . . We impressed, upon the minds of the more reflecting, the impropriety of having recourse to violence or coercion; and employed them in all directions, to counteract the intentions of those differently disposed. This influence we continued to exercise, until, one district giving way after another, the contest was finally given up about the end of February, 1813, having continued nine weeks; half of which time, the whole looms, engaged in the cotton manufacture in Scotland, (with a few trifling exceptions,) were at a stand.

ALEXANDER B. RICHMOND, *Narrative of the Condition of the Manufacturing Population* (1825)

5. Riots in Somersetshire, 1817

"(From a private Letter.)

Radstock, near Bath, March 2.

On Friday last, the colliers in the neighbourhood of Radstock and Paulton collected in a number of about three thousand, and manifested some very serious symptoms of riot and destruction to the pits and the buildings annexed to them, which spread the greatest consternation through the whole neighbourhood. Sir John Hippisley, accompanied by his brother magistrates, and several gentlemen, repaired to the spot, where he pointed out to them, in an impressive speech, the enormity of their offence. He read the Riot Act: it had no effect. They then proceeded, and took possession of several of the works, and sent persons down into the pits to compel those who worked in them to be drawn up, and then administered an oath not to work any more until their grievances were redressed, and threatened that night to demolish the works. Sir John and the magistrates sent immediately for a troop of the 23rd Lancers at Bristol, and the North Somerset Yeomanry, part of which arrived, and kept order for that night, and by day-break the whole of the North Somerset Yeomanry were on parade at Stone-Easton-house, and other places pointed out to them, so as to render assistance at every point where danger was apprehended. About nine o'clock Sir John Hippisley, accompanied by a numerous assemblage of magistrates and gentlemen, proceeded to Paulton, where these men were said to be, who, on hearing of the approach of the military, retired to Clandown coal-pits, and being pursued, retired to Radstock, where they made a stand, well furnished with immense bludgeons, and on seeing the cavalry approaching, gave three cheers, and called out, 'Bread or Blood; Hunt for ever!' The cavalry here came up, and filing off to the right and left, surrounded them, when Sir John Hippisley and the magistrates came into the centre, and addressed them to the following effect: — He wished to know what they wanted? They replied, 'full wages, and that they

11

were starving.' Sir John informed them, that the mode they had now adopted, by thus unlawfully assembling, was the very way to prevent any grievances they complained of being attended to: that he and his brother magistrates were determined to do their duty, and do it they would. Sir John stated to them, he was well informed, and knew, that their minds were inflamed by the disaffected, not only in speeches, but by parodies on the liturgy of the church, endeavouring not only to seduce them from their King, but from their God.

Previous to Sir John Hippisley's reading the riot act, he informed these infatuated men, that if they continued and remained one hour after the act was read, it would subject every person remaining to the sentence of death. He then read the riot act, when four of the principal of these deluded men were secured, and sent to Ilchester prison, escorted by a detachment of the North Somerset yeomanry cavalry, when the remainder dispersed.

It has been deemed necessary to station part of the 23d dragoons at Paulton and Radstock, and the yeomanry will be kept on duty for a few days longer on their respective parades.

Sir John then, in a speech to the yeomanry, by the request of the magistrates and gentlemen present, returned them sincere thanks for the alacrity with which they assembled, and expatiated on the utility of this valuable description of force; and was happy in being able to assert from the first authority, that the yeomanry would be considered as forming a part of the peace establishment: 'To you, Gentlemen of the North Somerset Yeomanry, it would be utterly impossible for me to give that well-earned and merited praise you are so justly entitled to on this as on all former occasions; your appearance and steadiness under arms has been acknowledged by all the general officers under whom you have done your duty. The thanks you have so often received from the general of the district, the corporations of Bath and Bristol, the lieutenancy and magistrates of this county, are a convincing proof of your value.'

Another Account. – A tumultuous and disorderly proceeding commenced on February 28th, amongst the colliers at Paulton, who, in consequence of an arrangement amounting to a reduction

12

of one-tenth of their wages, refused to work. This irregular step was but too readily followed by the miners in several of the neighbouring collieries, who, being assembled in considerable numbers, were collectively and most impressively addressed by that active magistrate, Sir J. Cox Hippisley, Bart. but they did not seem disposed to separate until the riot act had been read; in consequence of which they dispersed, and order seems completely restored. A reward of 20 guineas is offered for the discovery of the principal mover of this most ill-advised procedure. – *Bath Chronicle.*

Paulton, Tuesday night, March 4.
– It is with great pleasure we state, that all the colliers in this and the neighbouring mines are pursuing their usual employment with great satisfaction and content; and it is hoped and believed that their late misconduct is now become matter of most serious regret. A number of most inflammatory publications had been sold by a higgler at Paulton (where the mischief originated.) The leaders were arrested; but the poor wretches who followed them, we believe, were perfectly innocent of any bad design. We would, however, caution them to avoid those blasphemous and seditious publications which have caused their riotous conduct; and recommend them to look to their masters as their best friends. We are assured that there is not a collier-master in Somerset who at present puts a penny a year in his pocket; they must lose at the reduced prices, but they look forward to better times. – *Ditto.*"

Annual Register, 1817

6. Wool-Combers of Bradford, 1825

[*THE Combination Acts were repealed in 1824 and the repeal was the signal for widespread strikes. By the end of 1825 however the strike movement was arrested as a period of bad trade and irregular employment set in. Typical of the strikes of this period was the one described below.*]

CLASS-WAR IN BRADFORD

"Owing to the introduction of superior wools into the worsted trade, many changes had taken place in the conditions of wool-combing in the district, and the combers considered themselves entitled to certain concessions which the masters were not disposed to comply with. The disaffection spread to the weavers and the two classes of operatives ultimately combined, and on their demands being rejected by the masters they turned out and there commenced one of the bitterest struggles ever entered upon between employers and employed. Each week the breach seemed to widen, and both sides kept up the contest with dogged obstinacy and endurance, the workpeople being determined to enforce an advance, and the masters being equally resolute in their determination to break down the protective organisation arrayed against them. It is estimated that when the strike was at its height there were not less than twenty to thirty thousand people out of employment. The chief demand of the combers was "for combing low sorts of wool, such as britch, and low warp and weft, an advance of a farthing, and a halfpenny per pound where fine wool was not combed, and a halfpenny per pound where the low sorts were broken out of the finer fleeces," which meant an advance of from two to three shillings a week. It was contended by the masters that they were paying higher prices then for combing than had been paid for many years previously. The attitude of the masters

14

is shown in the fact that in the case of children employed at their works they dismissed all of them whose parents were in the Union, or who refused to sign a document declaring "that they had not joined the Union or any other society, nor would pay into any society to combine against their masters to raise wages." Very few, however, signed this declaration. From time to time the workpeople held meetings at Fairweather Green, near Bradford, at which speeches of a violent character were indulged in and resolutions passed expressing the determination of the men not to return to their work until their demands were fully complied with. The masters on their part declared that the demands of the men were altogether unreasonable and not justified by the condition of trade, and sought through the intercession of Mr. Wortley, M.P. to obtain a re-enactment of the Combination Laws. That gentleman had an interview with Mr. Secretary Peel on the subject, but the Government refused to interfere further than to promise to bring forward a measure increasing the penalties for assaults and threats by Unionists against Non-Unionists. While performing this service for the masters, however, Mr. Wortley took occasion to ask the master manufacturers of Bradford to consider whether it would not be wiser, instead of refusing to listen to any proposals coming from a committee of the workmen and acting for them (however it might be constituted), to grant them at once every point which upon a full consideration might appear reasonable. But although the masters received the delegates of the workpeople and listened to their representations, it was impossible for any compromise to be arrived at, seeing that not one of the demands of the strikers was regarded by the masters as reasonable . . ."

JAMES BURNLEY, *The History of Wool and Wool-combing* (1889)

THE PROGRESS OF THE STRIKE

". . . The first open act of the workmen, who had previously formed a Union among themselves, showed itself in their demanding a conference with the masters. Accordingly, on Monday, the 6th of

15

June, 1825, the masters assembled at the Sun Inn, Bradford, to the number of about thirty, and chose Mr. Matthew Thompson as chairman. The combers and weavers were represented by two delegates:— John Tester, who afterwards played so large a part in the strike, attended on behalf of the combers. . . .

As their demands were not acceded to . . . the combers next day, (Tuesday, 7th June) struck work against three firms in Bradford, Messrs. John Wroe and Sons, Messrs. Margerison and Peckover, and Messrs. Leach and Cousen. The following day the masters, to the number of fifty, held a meeting at the Sun Inn, Bradford, to consult on this emergency, when it was unanimously resolved, that, — It appeared from evidence, the prices for combing were higher than they had been for the last ten or twenty years, and provisions more reasonably than had often been the case during that period, and that the workmen's request was unreasonable. The resolution was somewhat modified respecting the weavers, but the meeting pledged itself not to employ any comber or weaver belonging to the *Union*. Thus the rupture became complete, and henceforward for the next twenty-two weeks a struggle commenced, which in its magnitude, the loss entailed, and calamitous results, is almost without parallel in the records of industry. The 'turn-outs' met weekly at Fairweather Green to listen to the reports and speeches of their leader, who declared, that until the demands of the workmen, to the full extent, met with compliance, they would never return to their work, and this threat, it seemed at the time would be carried into effect, inasmuch as numerous contributions poured in from all parts of the country. Delegates were sent to the principal manufacturing towns of the kingdom to induce the artisans to assist their Bradford fellows in resisting what was termed the oppression of the masters. After many fruitless conferences between the masters and the men, the former determined upon taking a very decided step, for the purpose of breaking up the Union, and at a meeting resolved to stop their mills on the 5th or 6th of August following. There were present thirty-nine masters, thirty-three of whom voted for the stoppage, and six against it.

To justify the measures they had adopted, the masters published a kind of manifesto . . . the most interesting portion (of which) . . . consists of the statement, that weaving by power-looms had come into competition with hand-loom weaving, and that the work by the former method progressively increased, and was of better quality and much cheaper. . . .

Before the middle of September there were unmistakeable signs of the combination not being so strong as previously. The subscriptions began to fall off; and the stuff markets being dull beyond precedent, the employers were not desirous of extending their operation. . . .

At last the Bradford workmen finding that their funds were failing, and that the state of the trade would not permit the masters to advance wages, began to yield. An interview took place, on Saturday, the 5th of November, between some of the workmen and Messrs. John Wood and John Rand, which, owing to the conciliatory conduct of the masters, resulted in seventy combers of the best character obtaining work at Mr. Wood's factory, and on the ensuing Monday there was a general resumption of labour to the extent of the masters' wants. Thus after a protracted struggle of twenty-two weeks, the workmen, as is usual in these cases, had to succumb, and under circumstances less favourable than when it commenced; for the trade of the district had become so shaken, and the pressure of the times so great, that for the ensuing twelve months the workmen endured many privations."

JOHN JAMES, *History of the Worsted Manufacturers in England* (1857)

17

7. The Swing Riots of 1830

[*IN 1830 there was widespread rioting, rick-burning and destruction of farm machinery throughout the Southern counties of England, when desperate farm labourers sought a remedy for their extreme poverty. Threatening letters signed "Swing" were received by many farmers and landowners. This gave the name to a campaign, which the Hammonds have termed "The Last Labourers' Revolt."*]

"Being at Winchester the other day, I returned to Andover— The regular distance being about eleven miles – by way of Sutton Scotney, which made the distance four miles farther. Sutton Scotney is a goodly-sized village – a thousand people in it, or thereabout. It has the village of Newton, in which parish it stands, half-a-mile eastward, and Barton Stacey, a parochial village, a mile westward. It was in these villages conjointly that the Swing riots of 1830 first began. Several persons belonging to them were convicted and transported, and one hanged. One of those who had been sentenced to seven years' transportation, but got off with two years' imprisonment at Portsmouth, was mentioned to me, and I sent for him, and drew him into familiar conversation. His account was to the following effect:–

"My name? my name be's Joseph Carter, Ees, I had seven year on't for them mobs; but they let me off with imprisonment at the hulks for two years and one day. That was the exact time. The way I got off was this – they found out when they put me to school there that I never could read none; no reading nor writing. I never had a book put afore me never in my life, not as I minds on, till I went aboard ship a prisoner to serve my seven year at Portsmouth. . . . But they finding out as how I had never been no scholard, they knew it could not have been I as old Barrowman called in to see if it wor a good ten-pound note. That old Barrowman was the father

18

of young Barrowman as was hanged. The old one was transported. Both they were from Barton Stacey.

"Well, about the ten-pound note, it was in this here way. The mob goes up to Mr Callander — he is Sir Thomas Baring's steward — and they said they must have money, or they would do mischief. Well, he said, don't do mischief, come in with me and I will give you money. Old Barrowman went in to get the money: but he could not read a word of figures or writing, and he did not know if it wor a good note. So he comes out and gets another man to go in with him, to see if the note wor a good one. Mack was the man who went in. He be here now, and everybody knows he wor the man as went in. But he be a tall man like myself; and, i' faith, somebody swore it wor me; and they took me. But when they found I wor no scholard, they believed it might not be me.

"Oh, ees, ees, I wor with them. But then, everybody was forced like to go. There was no denying. I be an old man now. I was not young then. It was the young men as did it. They worked, you see, for little wages, as they do now. They suffers most. They get but 4s., and 4s. 6d., and 5s., and one or two may get 5s. 6d. a-week. At that time the married men got 9s. and 10s. a-week. But it was the young men as led the others and forced them into it. I was took afore Squire Wickham and the other gentlemen, for the squire to shew as how I had no business to be mobbing. I was a hurdle maker and thatcher, and jobbed at hedging. The squire shewed as how I got L.64 a-year from him for work of that kind for seven years. But then he did not shew that I had most times a man to help me, and two women besides at times. He did not shew that. I paid as much as L.20 some years for helpers. Oh, I did not say I paid the money away that way, because they would ha' thought I complained, and would ha' taken that as guilty of going out to mob. I said that I wor forced out agin my will. And so I wor . . . I wor at the meeting across the street there . . . the night Joe Mason read the letter to us all . . . It said we was all to leave off work: and the Sutton men was to go out and stop the ploughs. They was to send home the horses for the farmers to look after them themselves, and was to take the men with them. And they was to go and turn the

19

men out of the barns. And they was all to go and break the 'sheens' as the farmers had got to do the thrashing . . .

"Well; about the letter. Joe Mason read it. We did not then know who it came from. But we knows, all on us now in this here place, that old D—s had a hand in't . . .

"About the letter; well, it was this: I was there at the reading on't, and that came all out, and you see that went agin me. And then some of them told as how that I carried the money; and, ecod, you see that was true. Joe Mason was by far the best scholard, but they would not trust Joe with the money; nor yet old Barrowman. They said I wor honest, and they gave it to me to carry. I had L.40 at one time – L.40 every shilling. Some people ha' told me since that I should ha' gone off with it. I did think of doing that once. The coach came by when we was up on the London Road, and it did come into my head to get on the coach, and get away from the whole business, with the L.40. But I thought about leaving my wife behind, and about what a vagabond they would all call me, and the coach was soon past. I never had another chance. But had I ha' knowed I was to be tried, and sentenced to be transported, I'd ha' got up on the coach.

"I needn't ha' been tried at all. They came to me times and times after I was in Winchester gaol, to get me to speak against the two Masons. They offered to let me clear, if I would only tell what I knowed agin them. Had I told what I knowed, they'd ha' been hung, as sure as Barrowman, and Cooke, and Cooper, was hung. I was took out with the other prisoners to see they hung. They tried to frighten us by it to tell all we knowed on one another. But I wouldn't split. So the Masons was only transported, and they transported me, too.

"Ees; the mob took me agin my will; but then that was not enough to make me split, 'cause you see, I stayed with them. They took many a man agin his will. They took Harry Mills of Barton Stacey, and carried him a mile and a half. Harry Mills be alive now. He wor yesterday. I seed him in this here place. He have a pension of one shilling a-day, he have. He wor in the 63d regiment, and stood guard over Bonaparte at St Helena. The mob carried Harry

Mills a mile and a half, and forced him to go with them. It wor the young fellows did it. The worst on them never got nothing done to them. Some of those as got most done to them, some as got hanged, never done half so much as some I knows on in this here parish." . . .

"What kind of food had you on board the hulk at Portsmouth the two years and a day you were there?"

"Why, sir, not always good alike; and not always bad alike. The bread was mostly always bad, 'cause one man who had great favour, had the contract all the time I was there. The butchers took the contract for six months; and there was a great deal of difference in one six months from another six months, according as to who might have the contract. The worst on't was better than I can get now in Sutton Scotney. I do not mean but there be's good meat to be got in Sutton by them as have money; but it ben't no working man like me as can get it. I wish I had as much meat now as I had in the hulk; and I wishes the same to every poor hard-working man in Hampshire.

"The allowance we had, sir, was this:— We had four ounces of biscuit a-day — the best of biscuit. The bread was one pound; it was black, and not good. We had oatmeal too, and pea soup; and we had garden vegetables that we bought with the money we worked for. We had fourteen ounces of meat each time, four times a-week; one six months the meat was beautiful. That man gave always good meat when he had the contract. We had plenty of victuals. The only thing was the bread. I wishes every poor, hard-working man in this here parish were as well fed with meat, and myself with them, as I wor in the hulk." . . ."

ALEXANDER SOMERVILLE, *The Whistler at the Plough* (Manchester, 1852)

8. The Derby Movement, 1833-4

[*THE repeal of the Combination Laws (1824/5) naturally resulted in growing activity of the unions which extended throughout the country. This received a new impetus in 1833 by the establishment of a trade-union newspaper called* The Pioneer. *The following editorial from the issue of 11th January, 1834, deals with the decision of employers in Derby to "lock-out" trade union members.*]

"The master manufacturers of Derby have repeated their *"firm* and *inflexible* determination not to employ any men who belong to the Trades' Union, or of any other Union, having similar objects."

Now we would ask these master manufacturers what they expect to be the result of these proceedings? The one of two things is evident; either the men will be forced into tame submission, by want, or they will be able, by the assistance of their fellow-workmen, and other benevolent persons, to establish machinery, &c., of their own. If they be reduced to the former alternative, it will be by sheer force, under the garb of deprivation. But the day of retribution, blackened by the remembrance of manifold wrongs, will sooner or later arrive; for no means have been taken to show cause why this damnable tyranny should be enacted, and the momentary triumph would be the harbinger of reckless, hopeless, grim despair. Operatives of England! these foolish men have collected a tissue of falsehoods, to prove to the public that you can at any time, by prompt coercion, be forced into submission. They treat us like Helots, who are doomed to bear perpetual bondage; they descend not to reason with us; they show us no commiseration; nor do they esteem us as fellow-creatures. It is well that we are of the same colour, or probably they would adopt the lash. They despise the law of unity and progression, and expect to

22

succeed. The experiment was tried on the labourers, and the sky was illumined with blazing produce. God forbid that the operative, with his present skill and intelligence, should be forced to act the demon. We pause for breath. Once rob the operative of his self-esteem; once take away his honest pride. A slave ye cannot make him now; but force him to a slave's condition, and where is your security? How far, and please your honours, must competition go? To what low depth of degradation must we descend, before your eyes are cleansed from error? How many bended knees will satiate your *firmness* and *inflexibility?* How many children should you like to perish? How many graves with carrion crammed? How much of suffering will suffice to soothe your pride? Shall we, your friend, the *Pioneer,* consume our manuscripts, and offer you our neck? Good, gentle masters, do have mercy! your power is infinite; but, O be merciful! Your names shall be inscribed in dead men's bones, to blazen your omnipotence; and broken hearts shall be inurned to make men dread your power. We shall petition for enactment to give you liberty to whip us; nay, you shall wear a dagger in your girdles, to rip our humble bowels up; and last, not least, shall have the aid of reverend priests to damn our souls to all eternity.

Brave fellow-workmen, are you ripe for this? Have you made up your minds to put your souls and bodies in your masters' keeping? If not, then lend a friend your ear. Prepare your hands for an united effort and temporary sacrifice; cease all complaints; use not an angry word; forget all selfishness; and do your best to blast these rich men's hopes, and set the Derby men to work. Give up your mites with that express condition; it will not do to waste a penny. To work they must. Our Labour Fund must not be spent in idleness. The Derby men must look to this; let no man be ashamed to turn his hand, till means are ready. The time and circumstances do make it virtuous; and if they are not worthy of this trial, the means must be reserved for those who are. Derby may fail, by indiscretion — the cause of truth can never die. These cruel purse-proud men are not infallible, and kings have tumbled from their thrones. It will be hard then, and black disgrace, if union cannot thwart their purpose. The proper men must form a work-committee, and a labour bank, whose funds shall be held sacred for that sole purpose, to set the men to work; old strikes must pass away, and men must learn to manage capital. Thousands would help in such a cause as this, that would not give a doit to struggle vainly with a master's purse, and gain no object . . ."

The Pioneer (January 1834)

[Contributions for *The Derby List* poured into the offices of *The Pioneer* for months to come. A typical list below.]

THE DERBY LIST

Subscriptions received at the Pioneer Office, London

A few Tailors, at the White Hart, Little Windmill-street, per W. Boatman	£ 1	12	9
John Ede, an Enemy to Tyranny	0	0	6
Branch Lodge, No. 1, of the F.S.O.C., held at the Duchess of Clarence, Vauxhall-bridge-road, Voluntary Subscription	4	1	0
A few initiated Tailors, and Friends in the City	0	4	5
From the Journeymen, at No. 20, Cork-street, J. Brown, Sec.	0	13	3
No. 5, Branch Lodge of F.S.O.C., a 2d. counter-shot	1	14	7
No. 1 Lodge, Smith's Union, 8 Theobald's-road, by George Tomey	0	1	0
Joseph George, Shoemaker, by ditto	0	1	0
A few brother Carpenters and Friends, No. 2 Branch Lodge, Clarendon Arms, Camberwell, Surrey	1	12	6
Leather-dressers' Union, Bermondsey	7	1	10
Brotherly Operative Bricklayers of London	27	10	0
Sons of Freedom at the Fox Tavern, Russell-street, Whitechapel-road, Mile-end	1	15	0
A few Republican Friends, Cock Inn, Clapham, Surrey	0	11	3

9. The Tolpuddle Martyrs, 1834

THE DORCHESTER LABOURERS

"IT happened that a poor labouring man, named Loveless, living in a small village in Dorsetshire, was, in the year 1834, in great distress. He had a family, and had hitherto supported them by his small earnings of seven shillings a-week. This sum was about to be reduced to six shillings, and the poor man saw that the little comforts he had been able to gain for his wife and children out of this seven shillings (and God knows that these comforts must have been small) were about to be taken from him by such a diminution of his wages.

In his distress, he writes to his brother, living in London, and tells him his situation and his fears. His brother writes in answer, that in London the labouring men had devised a means to prevent the lowering of their wages.

The poor labourer of Dorsetshire (Loveless) was well known to his brother to be an honest, upright, and peaceable man, – one who willingly would not break the law – and his brother, therefore, was careful while explaining the means used by the labouring men of London to avert the lowering of their wages, to point out that their scheme was a perfectly legal one. He told him that their mode was to form an association, called a Trades' Union; to make certain rules for their guidance; and, at the same time, he explained the use of the Union to the labouring men. He then said that these Unions had been in existence nearly four months: that their existence was well known to the authorities in London; and that no opposition had been made to them by the legal officers of the crown. They had processions, he said; they were in the habit, daily, of acting together as unionists; and they (the men) expected much good from the association.

The poor country labourers determined to adopt the plan of their brethren in London.

Three of the Martyrs: from Cleave's Penny Gazette of Variety, 1838.

There was, however, one circumstance in the situation of the country labourer that surrounded him with difficulties unknown to the working-man of London. The poor men of a village are few; they are scattered; and every action they perform is known to their masters. In London great numbers may unite, and, by their very numbers, place themselves in a position to be respected by their masters. In London they did not so much dread the masters, and therefore did not seek or need concealment. In the country they had no numbers to defend one another, and the poor men, therefore, sought to shelter themselves by concealment. In an evil hour for themselves *they formed a secret association.*

Thus far, however, they proceeded with perfect legality.

They had a right to associate for the purpose of maintaining or raising the rate of their wages.

They had a right, if it so pleased them, to form a secret association.

But, unfortunately, they determined TO SWEAR ONE ANOTHER TO SECRECY.

Six of these men were informed by the constable of the village, that there was a charge against them at Dorchester, and requested them to go there with him and answer it. The poor fellows, believing themselves perfectly innocent, told the constable they would go with him; and informed their wives and families that they would be back in the evening. *The poor men never returned!*

Arrived at Dorchester, they found a body of magistrates, who took depositions against them, and sent them to gaol, remanding them to the next Saturday, the day on which they were first examined being Tuesday. The magistrates, when the Saturday came, finished the examination in the gaol and in secret, and they were finally committed for trial.

CAUTION.

WHEREAS it has been represented to us from several quarters, that mischievous and designing Persons have been for some time past, endeavouring to induce, and have induced, many Labourers in various Parishes in this County, to attend Meetings, and to enter into Illegal Societies or Unions, to which they bind themselves by unlawful oaths, administered secretly by Persons concealed, who artfully deceive the ignorant and unwary,—WE, the undersigned Justices think it our duty to give this PUBLIC NOTICE and CAUTION, that all Persons may know the danger they incur by entering into such Societies.

ANY PERSON who shall become a Member of such a Society, or take any Oath, or assent to any Test or Declaration not authorized by Law—

Any Person who shall administer, or be present at, or consenting to the administering or taking any Unlawful Oath, or who shall cause such Oath to be administered, although not actually present at the time—

Any Person who shall not reveal or discover any Illegal Oath which may have been administered, or any Illegal Act done or to be done—

Any Person who shall induce, or endeavour to persuade any other Person to become a Member of such Societies,

WILL BECOME

Guilty of Felony,

AND BE LIABLE TO BE

Transported for Seven Years.

ANY PERSON who shall be compelled to take such an Oath, unless he shall declare the same within four days, together with the whole of what he shall know touching the same, will be liable to the same Penalty.

Any Person who shall directly or indirectly maintain correspondence or intercourse with such Society, will be deemed Guilty of an Unlawful Combination and Confederacy, and on Conviction before one Justice, on the Oath of one Witness, be liable to a Penalty of TWENTY POUNDS, or to be committed to the Common Gaol or House of Correction, for THREE CALENDAR MONTHS; or if proceeded against by Indictment, may be CONVICTED OF FELONY, and be TRANSPORTED FOR SEVEN YEARS.

Any Person who shall knowingly permit any Meeting of any such Society to be held in any House, Building, or other Place, shall for the first offence be liable to the Penalty of FIVE POUNDS; and for every other offence committed after Conviction, be deemed Guilty of such Unlawful Combination and Confederacy, and on Conviction before one Justice, on the Oath of one Witness, be liable to a Penalty of TWENTY POUNDS, or to Commitment to the Common Gaol or House of Correction, FOR THREE CALENDAR MONTHS; or if proceeded against by Indictment may be

CONVICTED OF FELONY,
And Transported for SEVEN YEARS.

COUNTY OF DORSET. Dorchester Division	C. B. WOLLASTON, JAMES FRAMPTON, WILLIAM ENGLAND, THOS. DADE, JNO. MORTON COLSON,	HENRY FRAMPTON, RICHD. TUCKER STEWARD, WILLIAM R. CHURCHILL, AUGUSTUS FOSTER.
February 22d, 1834		

G. CLARK, PRINTER, CORNHILL, DORCHESTER.

27

When the trial came on it was found that they were indicted under an almost forgotten statute made against seditious meetings, the 32 Geo. III. c. 104. In the body of the Act was a provision making it an offence subject to transportation, to administer an oath at any meeting held for an unlawful purpose; and the men indicted (under this portion of the Act) were for having administered oaths at an unlawful meeting.

For an unauthorized person to administer an oath is, by the common law, an offence, a misdemeanour — but this offence can be visited only by a common-law punishment; transportation is not a common-law punishment — therefore some statute is required to allow the infliction of the punishment of transportation.

To bring the administering of the oath by these labourers to one another, within the grasp of those who desired to transport them, it was therefore requisite to prove, not merely that they had committed an offence against the common law, but also against some express statute. The statute selected for this purpose was the one I have above-mentioned.*

Before the men, however, could be brought within this statute it was necessary to show that the *intent* of the meeting was an *unlawful* intent.

But the intent was a perfectly lawful one. A few years since, indeed, it was an offence in labourers to combine together for the purpose of raising or maintaining the rate of wages. But this law, atrocious in every sense of the term, was repealed, and it is now perfectly lawful for labourers to combine to maintain their wages, and to protect themselves: *provided that they do not violently coerce or intimidate any one.*

The Grand Jury, however, found a true bill against the men. The Petty Jury convicted them, and the Judge sentenced them to seven years' transportation.

An objection was taken at the trial as to the propriety of the verdict. Petitions were immediately presented to the Home Office, stating that serious doubts were entertained as to the legality of the sentence, and praying for a remission of it. Their case was also mentioned in Parliament as one of peculiar hardship, and time was

* There were no less than five Acts of Parliament dug up for the purpose of finding something on which to found the condemnation of these men.

asked to learn whether they were legally convicted. Everything was refused. The men were hurried out of the country, and the unsuspecting, and as far as intention was concerned, innocent men, who had left their native village in the perfect confidence that they should rest that same night under their own roof-tree, in a few weeks found themselves floating upon the waters, transported convicts.

Petition upon petition was presented to Parliament. The labouring population from one end of the kingdom to the other was roused and irritated. A sense of insecurity pervaded the people. Injustice had been done, and no one knew, but that he might undergo the same fate. All this, in the opinion of Parliament, signified nothing; it was necessary to terrify the labouring classes; this blow was given to that end; so they were determined to let the innocent suffer.

Things were mentioned in Parliament as aggravating this offence, which deserve to be recorded in the hearts and memories of the English people. They should be known to all of them, and handed down as a legacy to the children who shall succeed them. The time may come when, by some, it may be wished that they were buried in oblivion.

I pursue the narrative of this case however, rapidly and briefly in order that I may come to the late discussion respecting it. The objections made against mercy were then again repeated, and may as well be answered once for all.

A year has passed away, and the people have not forgotten their suffering brethren. The feeling of commiseration for their lot is as warm now as when they were first convicted. Though far off, and many, many thousand miles of waste waters roll between us and them, the chain of sympathy is still unbroken. . . .

From one end of Britain to the other petitions have come up, and crowded the table of the House of Commons; the people have again forced the case before their so-called representatives, and again they have been taught by their conduct *that the House of Commons does not represent the feelings of the people.*"

J. A. ROEBUCK, M.P. (1835)

THE PROCESSION
Of the Workmen of London, to save their Dorchester Brethren.

They smote — we saw our brethren fall,
    Struck by the foeman's dart;
The blow they suffer'd wounded *all* —
    'Twas felt in every heart.

Base despots! who deal deadly words
    In cunning guise of law,
Trust ye to jargon and to swords
    Our souls to overawe?

We rend your veil, we scorn your steel;
    We shrink not nor dissemble —
By every burning wrong we feel,
    Cold tyrants! ye shall tremble.

We moved, — a calm majestic mass, —
    In silence and in power,
And never from men's hearts shall pass
    The lesson of that hour.

In our arms that idly hung,
    Slumber'd strength that shall not tire —
In our silence was a tongue
    Which, though mute, spoke words of fire.

And did our foes not *feel* that day,
    Howe'er they may dissemble —
Did not our firm and cool array
    Make tyrants' bosoms tremble?

Hence, paltry threat and pity vile,
    The froth and slime of slaves —
Freedom and Right shall bless our toil,
    Or shine upon our graves!

From *The Gathering of the Unions* (sold by
Cleave, 1 Shoe Lane, London, 1834)

10. The Power of Strikes, 1834

"THEIRS will not be insurrection; it will be simply passive resistance. The men may remain at leisure; there is, and can be, no law to compel them to work against their will. They may walk the streets or fields with their arms folded, they will wear no swords, carry no muskets, assemble no train of artillery, seize upon no fortified places. They will present no column for an army to attack, no multitude for the Riot-Act to disperse. They merely abstain, when their funds are sufficient, from going to work for one week, or one month, through the three kingdoms. And what happens in consequence? *Bills are dishonoured, the Gazette teems with bankruptcies, capital is destroyed, the revenue fails, the system of Government falls into confusion,* and every link in the chain which binds society together is broken in a moment by this inert conspiracy of the poor against the rich."

From *The Liberator* (organ of the Trades'
Unions of Scotland, 1st February, 1834)

11. The Evils of Strikes, 1838

". . . THE Committee of the Trades Unions . . . imperiously command not only the members of their own Combination, but all other workmen whatever, from any quarter, from infringing upon, or interfering with that state of compulsory idleness. This deplorable state of matters, too, is not produced by a numerical majority of the whole human beings concerned. The skilled labourers, that is, a twentieth or thirtieth part of the mass, alone are consulted; and a majority of them in the first instance adopt the fatal step. After it is adopted, and the committee organized, the power even of that small majority is at an end. It in itself has fallen under the dominion of the committee of its own creating, which is in possession of the public funds; which feels none of the penury shared by the general body; which is invested with money to hire assassins, and armed with the terrors of murder, fire-raising, and vitriolic acid. For months before the strike terminates, the great majority even of the skilled workmen who authorized it, have come heartily to repent of their folly; they secretly lament their unhappy blindness, and execrate the leaders who advised them to the fatal step; but they dare not venture to give breath in public to these sentiments, and in sullen mournful silence continue to yield unwilling obedience to the mandates of the Secret Ruling Committee. Mean-while, their families are reduced to the last stages of destitution; multitudes are perishing for want; licentiousness arises out of idleness; crime out of suffering; fever and pestilence make fearful inroads on a depressed and extenuated population, until at length the miseries and lamentations of the starving multitude compel the Committee to abandon the contest, and permit the joyful sounds of industry and happiness again to be heard through the land."

Trades' Unions and Strikes (*Edinburgh Review*, April, 1838)

12. The Lanarkshire Iron-Workers, 1837

HOW THE LANARKSHIRE IRON-MASTERS
CUT THEIR COSTS IN 1837

". . . IN LANARKSHIRE, in the course of the Spring of 1837, the iron-masters, in the extensive and increasing iron-establishments in that county, being unable, when iron had fallen from L.7 to L.4, 10s. a-ton, to continue the extravagant wages of thirty-five shillings a-week for fifteen hours' work, began to take in new hands from the starving weavers, who, at that period, were reduced to the last stage of destitution. The whole colliers, upon this, immediately struck work, and began to assault the new hands. These proceedings, however, were checked by stationing soldiers at Airdrie, – the centre of the iron-works – in the beginning of May, where they remained till the end of August; and by establishing a strong police force, which the masters paid, and equipped at their own expense, and kept at the works; and by the instant seizure and summary punishment of some of the colliers who had commenced the plan of assault and intimidation. The consequence was, that the new hands, being protected, continued their labours, and their numbers were increased; and the starving weavers, during the commercial distress, found a most seasonable relief from the insane strike of the colliers.

These weavers soon acquired considerable proficiency, and at the *end of a few months, were making five shillings a-day,* in place of tenpence, which the few who could find employment were only able to earn at their former trade. The consequence was, that the combined colliers were compelled in the end to give in; that they now work five days in the week instead of three, and eight hours a-day instead of four; and the result has been, that though trade has improved since coals were so extravagantly high, they have already fallen from sixteen shillings a-ton to thirteen shillings. But nevertheless, had it not been that there were troops at

33

hand, and that the iron-masters had the courage and spirit to raise and equip a body of forty policemen, and to maintain them at their own expense for six months, there can be no doubt that the combination would have proved successful; — that the iron-masters would have been compelled to give, during a period of unexampled distress, the same rate of wages which they had given during one of unprecedented prosperity; — and that they must either have given over working their vast iron-works altogether, or become bankrupt . . ."

Trades' Unions and Strikes (*Edinburgh Review,*
April, 1838)

13. Glasgow Cotton Spinners Strike, 1837

A HOSTILE VIEW

". . . THE number of spinners in Glasgow in April, 1837, was between eight and nine hundred; and the piecers and pickers, carders and reelers dependent on their labour, about seven times as many. During the extravagant prosperity of the summer of 1836, the spinners had memorialized the masters for an advance of wages in consequence of the rise in the price of cotton goods which then took place. The wages of the spinners before this rise were from thirty to thirty-five shillings a week; and after the rise, which the masters agreed to, they were from thirty-five to forty-two. In consequence, however, of the commercial crisis of January and February 1837, prices fell so much that it became necessary to recall this advance; and the masters proposed in March 1837 that wages should be restored to their previous rate. Even at the reduced rates the spinners might make from twenty-six to thirty-six shillings a week. The workmen, however, unanimously refused to accede to these terms; and as the masters declined to give any higher, the former struck work in a body on 8th April, 1837. They did so on the avowed principle that they were entitled, and determined to keep up wages, during a period of unexampled gloom and depression, to the level which they had attained in one of unprecedented prosperity. . . .

The strike continued from the 8th of April, till the 5th of August, being a period of 17 weeks and five days. It terminated at last by the spinners unanimously agreeing to return to their work, within three days after the ruling committee had been arrested in a body for their alleged accession to the murder of Smith, in the streets of Glasgow, on 22nd July.

It may readily be conceived what must have been the sufferings of the operatives during the latter weeks of this disastrous strike. The aliment allowed by the Association to each man during the latter part of the strike was only *eighteenpence* a week. Such was the deplorable pittance to which the deluded operative was reduced, who refused, or was compelled by the committee to refuse during the whole time from thirty to thirty-five shillings a week! The condition of the female operatives — the piecers, pickers, carders, and reelers — was infinitely worse, for there was no fund whatever provided for *their* maintenance, and from the commencement they were thrown upon the streets without either asylum, employment, or subsistence. It may readily be conceived what must have been the consequence of six or seven thousand women being kept in a state of destitution and idleness for four months; especially when in close proximity to equal numbers of the other sex, also trained to disorderly habits by the habitual receipt of high wages and the practice of frequent intemperance. The necessary consequences was, that crime and immorality increased to a frightful degree; and the rapid progress of fever, as well as great increase in the rate of mortality, evinced, in an appalling manner, how fatal such *strikes* are to the best interests of the labouring poor."

Trades' Unions and Strikes (*Edinburgh Review,*
April, 1838)

14. The Newport Rising, 1839

[*AFTER the failure of the Reform Act of 1832 to give the vote to any substantial numbers of the working class, there arose a nation-wide movement for universal suffrage based on the six points of the People's Charter. Although there was much talk within the Chartist movement of the need for a national insurrection to gain the six points, the only armed movement of any importance made by the Chartists was the Newport rising. Some thousands of miners marched on Newport. They were met by a small group of soldiers who fired upon them and routed them. The leaders, including John Frost, formerly mayor of Newport, were arrested and tried for high treason.*]

JOHN FROST – CHARTIST

"The third day comes a frost, a killing frost,
And, – when he thinks good easy man, full surely
His greatness is a-ripening, – nips his root."

WILLIAM SHAKESPEARE (*Henry VIII*)

". . . The story of Frost's rising may be told very shortly. The area in which it was to begin was the hill district near Newport, Monmouth, between the rivers of the Rhymney and the Sirdowy, and the town itself, which stands upon the highway from South Wales to Bristol, Gloucester, and Birmingham, and to the North of England. Plans were laid for a general rising on Sunday, 3rd November, 1839, when the men who took part were to arm themselves and march in three divisions upon Newport. John Frost was to march from Blackwood, which lies between the rivers already named, at the head of one division, Zephaniah Williams, who lived higher up the country and kept a beer shop at Coalbrook Vale, near Nantyglo, was to lead the second, and the third division was

37

to be under the control of one William Jones, a watchmaker of Pontypool, who was to collect men from the North and East.

The three divisions were to meet near Risca, about five miles from Newport, at midnight, and to march so as to reach it about 2 a.m., when the inhabitants would be asleep, to attack and overcome the troops quartered in the town, to take possession of it and to break down the bridge which there crosses the river Usk at its mouth. By this latter act they would stop the mail to Birmingham from Bristol; and those in concert with them, upon the failure of the mail to reach Birmingham at the time it was due, would thus learn that the rising and attack upon Newport had been successful. Thence the message would be sent throughout the Midlands and to the North. There was thereupon to be a general rising throughout Lancashire and the country generally. Charter Law was to be universally and instantly established.

The scheme miscarried from the outset. The division under Williams did not arrive till after the mêlée described below had taken place; that under Jones was later and did not get beyond Malpas; and Frost's army was delayed long after the appointed time. However, Frost collected what men he could and marched upon Newport at dawn. In all he was accompanied by 5,000 men, some armed with guns and pistols, many with spears and pikes, others with mining pickaxes – and scythes fixed on poles, and sticks and bludgeons, were made to do duty for want of better offensive weapons.

This contingent marched as far as the Westgate Inn at the outskirts of the town. Thither some thirty soldiers under Lieutenant Gray were sent from the barracks to the assistance of the mayor, who had stationed police there and joined them himself. Frost learned that the inn was occupied by soldiers, and, failing to gain an entrance otherwise, he gave the order to fire upon the windows of the room where the soldiers were. The military returned the fire. Several fell wounded on either side, and one or more were killed. On this there was a speedy dispersion of the insurgents, who were scattered in all directions. Frost himself beat a retreat towards Tredegar Park, and was arrested in the evening at Newport, with loaded pistols and ammunition upon him."

[*The trial of John Frost began on 31st December, 1839*]

". . . Upon the facts above related, it was plain that many of the insurgents might have been prosecuted individually for crimes not uncommon in the criminal Courts; for murder or manslaughter, for injuries inflicted with intent to do grievous bodily harm, unlawful wounding, or the like; but it was deemed advisable to prosecute the ringleaders for the greatest offence known to law, high treason, otherwise they might have escaped from lack of evidence precise enough to convict them individually of their crimes.

The law of high treason depended then upon two Statutes, the one of the twenty-fifth year of Edward III (1352), the latter of the thirty-sixth year of George III (1796). The Chief Justice, in his charge, explained to the grand jury the scope and effect of these Statutes, and cited the authority of Lord Chief Justice Hale (1671) and Sir Michael Foster, explaining that:

'Every insurrection which in judgment of law is intended against the person of the King, whether to dethrone or imprison him, or to oblige him to alter his measures or government, or to remove evil counsellors from about him; all such risings amount to a levying of war within the Statute. So, insurrections to throw down all enclosures, to alter the established law or change religion, to enhance the price of labour, or to open all prisons; all risings in order to effect these innovations of a public and general concern by an armed force are, in construction of law, High Treason within the clause of levying war; for though not levelled at the person of the King, they are against his Royal Majesty; and, besides, they have a direct tendency to dissolve all the bonds of society, and to destroy all property and all government, too, by numbers and an armed force. Insurrections, likewise, for redressing national grievances, or for the reformation of real or imaginary evils of a public nature, and in which the insurgents have no special interest; risings to effect these ends by force and numbers are, by construction of law, within the clause of levying war, for they are levelled at the King's crown and royal dignity.' "

[John Frost was defended by Sir Frederick Pollock (from whose biography these extracts are made) who, relying on a purely technical point of law, saved his client from the death penalty. On the 1st February, 1840, the death sentences on Frost and two other leaders of the rising were commuted to transportation for life.]

LORD HANWORTH, *Lord Chief Justice Pollock*
— A Memoir by His Grandson (1929)

15. Strikes for the Charter, 1842

[ON 15th August, 1842, a conference of delegates from Yorkshire
and Lancashire trades was held in Manchester which called upon
the working-class throughout the country to hold a General Strike
for the People's Charter. The following resolution was passed:]

". . . That we, delegates representing the various trades of
Manchester and its vicinity, with delegates from various parts of
Lancashire and Yorkshire, do most emphatically declare that it
is our solemn and conscientious conviction that all the evils that
afflict society and which have prostrated the energies of the
great body of the producing classes, arise solely from class legislation and that the only remedy for the present alarming distress
and widespread destitution is the immediate and unmutilated
adoption and carrying into law of the document known as the
People's Charter. That this meeting recommend that the peoples
of all trades and callings forthwith cease work until the above
document becomes the law of the land."

They met again at the 16th to discuss further measures, but were
dispersed by the police; they managed to meet again on the same
day and issue the following appeal:

"To the Trades of Manchester and surrounding districts.

"We hasten to lay before you the paramount importance of
the day's proceedings. The delegates from the surrounding districts have been more numerous at this day's meeting than they
were at yesterday's; and the spirit of determination manifested
for the people's rights has increased every hour. In consequence
of the unjust and unconstitutional interference of the magistrates our proceedings were abruptly brought to a close by their
dispersing the meeting, but not until in their very teeth we
passed the following resolution:

" 'The delegates in public meeting assembled do recommend to the various constituencies which we represent to adopt legal means to carry into effect the People's Charter. And further we recommend that delegates be sent to the whole of the country to endeavour to obtain the co-operation of the middle and working classes in carrying out the resolution of ceasing labour until the Charter be the law of the land.'

"Englishmen! Legally determine to maintain the peace and the well-being of the country, and show, by the strict adherence to our resolutions, that we are your representatives."

ALEXANDER HUTCHINSON
CHARLES STUART.

Manchester, August 16, 1842."

[*On 17th August, 1842, the Executive Committee of the National Chartists' Association issued the following poster in Manchester for which their President, James Leach, was arrested.*]

ADDRESS OF THE EXECUTIVE COMMITTEE OF THE NATIONAL CHARTISTS' ASSOCIATION "TO THE PEOPLE"

"Brother Chartists — The great political truths which have been agitated during the last half-century have at length aroused the degraded and insulted white slaves of England to a sense of their duty to themselves, their children, and their country. Tens of thousands have flung down their implements of labour. Your task masters tremble at your energy, and expecting masses eagerly watch this the great crisis of our cause. Labour must no longer be the common prey of masters and rulers. Intelligence has beamed upon the mind of the bondsman, and he has been convinced that all wealth, comfort, and produce, everything valuable, useful, and elegant, have sprung from the palms of his hands; he feels that his cottage is empty, his back thinly clad, his children breadless, himself hopeless, his mind harassed, and his body punished, that undue riches, luxury, and gorgeous plenty might be heaped on the palaces of the taskmasters, and flooded in the granaries of the oppressor. Nature, God, and reason, have condemned this inequality, and in the thunder of a people's voice it must perish for ever. He knows that labour, the real property of society, the sole origin of accumulated property, the first cause of all national wealth, and the only supporter, defender, and contributor to the greatness of our country, is not possessed of the same legal protection which is given to those lifeless effects, the houses, ships, and machinery, which labour have alone created. He knows that if labour has no protection, wages cannot be upheld nor in the slightest degree regulated, until every workman of twenty-one years of age, and of sane mind, is on the same political level as the employer. He knows that the Charter would remove by universal will, expressed in universal suffrage, the heavy load of taxes which now crush the existence of the labourer, and cripple the efforts of commerce; that it would give cheap government as well as cheap food, high wages as well as low taxes, bring happiness to the hearthstone, plenty to the table, protection to the old, education to the young, permanent prosperity to the country, long continued protective political power to labour, and peace, blessed peace, to exhausted humanity and approving nations; therefore it is that we have solemnly sworn, and one and all declared, that the golden opportunity now within our grasp shall not pass away fruitless, that the chance of centuries afforded to us by a wise and all-seeing God, shall not be lost; but that we now do universally resolve never to resume labour until labour's grievances are destroyed, and protection secured for ourselves, our suffering wives, and helpless, children, by the enactment of the People's Charter.

Englishmen! the blood of your brothers reddens the streets of Preston and Blackburn, and the murderers thirst for more. Be firm, be courageous, be men. Peace, law, and order have prevailed on our side — let them be revered until your brethren in Scotland, Wales, and Ireland are informed of your resolution; and when the universal holiday prevails, which will be the case in eight days, then of what use will bayonets be against public opinion? What tyrant can then live above the terrible tide of thought and energy, which is now flowing fast, under the guidance of man's intellect, which is now destined by a Creator to elevate his people above the reach of want, the rancour of despotism, and the penalties of bondage. The trades, a noble, patriotic band, have taken the lead in declaring for the Charter, and drawing their gold from the keeping of tyrants. Follow their example. Lend no whip to rulers wherewith to scourge you.

Intelligence has reached us of the wide-spreading of the strike, and now, within fifty miles of Manchester, every engine is at rest, and all is still, save the miller's useful wheels and the friendly sickle in the fields.

Countrymen and brothers, centuries may roll on as they have fleeted past, before such universal action may again be displayed: we have made the cast for liberty, and we must stand, like men, the hazard of the die. Let none despond. Let all be cool and watchful; and, like the bridemaids in the parable, keep your lamps burning; and let continued resolution be like a beacon to guide those who are now hastening far and wide to follow your memorable example.

Brethren, we rely upon your firmness; cowardice, treachery, or womanly fear would cast our cause back for half a century. Let no man, woman, or child break down the solemn pledge, and if they do, may the curse of the poor and starving pursue them — they deserve slavery who would madly court it.

Our machinery is all arranged, and your cause will, in three days, be impelled onward by all the intellect we can summon to its aid; therefore, whilst you are peaceful, be firm; whilst you are orderly, make all be so likewise; and whilst you look to the law, remember that you had no voice in making it, and are therefore the slaves to the will, the law, and the price of your masters.

All officers of the association are called upon to aid and assist in the peaceful extension of the movement, and to forward all monies for the use of the delegates who may be expressed over the country. Strengthen our hands at this crisis. Support your leaders. Rally round our sacred cause, and leave the decision 'to the God of justice and of battle.' "

16. The Pottery Riots of 1842

"THESE began at Hanley on the 15th of August, 1842. A strike of colliers had occurred some weeks before. This event had deepened and intensified the general discontent and poverty of the whole district. People in large numbers were living on the verge of starvation. Some praiseworthy efforts were made to relieve this distress, but these were fitful and narrow in their scope. The only sure source of relief offered was one repulsive to the bulk of the sufferers — "The Bastile."* To this many were driven by dire necessity . . . At the time of which I write there was . . . rather a determination "to put down" the masses. The people, nevertheless, were willing to work. They were even anxious to work, as some years previously trade in the Potteries had been in a fairly flourishing condition, so far as the constancy of it had been concerned. With plenty of trade, however, the long hours of labour had tended to lengthen. Wages remained scanty, and as there was no effective trade-unionism the workers did not share in the improved profits, but simply got more abundant toil. When slackness came again, as it did about 1839, with this slackness came attempts even to reduce wages, increasing poverty and increasing exasperation of the people went hand in hand. This state of things produced a general condition of mind favourable to any change. Hopeless poverty is a fruitful soil for revolution. Chartism, just then rising into notoriety in the country, professed to be able to show the sure way to beneficent changes. The people had no power. The people must have power, and hence the "People's Charter", which gave assurance that all this, if loyally and generally supported, would make this a glorious fact. . . .

There was another cause which helped on the general discontent. While the employers were becoming increasingly rampant in their exactions, pressing the utmost hours of labour at the lowest prices, there were increasing signs on every hand of their growing

* The work-house.

45

wealth. Men who, a few years before, had been themselves workmen or small manufacturers were now becoming large manufacturers, building big houses, and surrounding themselves with luxuries and elegancies, which were the sure signs of growing wealth. These signs were coincident with the pleading of manufacturers of the need for lower wages. The result was a deepening sullenness, a deepening defiance over the whole district. This was the common mood when "the six points of the Charter" were brought forth like so many radiant finger-posts, pointing the people to a Land of Promise near at hand.

These were the conditions prevailing when the colliers' strike occurred in July 1842. The effect of this strike was to stop many of the pot-works for want of coal, and thus to aggravate the general distress and disaffection.

I have already told of the colliers coming to a colliery near Tunstall and breaking up everything breakable on the pit bank, when the poor constable was pitched into the pond near by, and shoved back with a rail when he came near the edge of the pond. That was an ominous sign of rougher work and wilder deeds soon to follow.

After Thomas Cooper's* harangues at the Crown Bank, Hanley, on the 14th of August, and on the following morning, at the same place, his fervid denunciation of the people's oppressors acted like a fell inspiration in the hearts of his hearers. As soon as Cooper had done speaking someone cried out, "Follow me." This invitation was loudly cheered and eagerly followed. The maddened crowd swept first across the Crown Bank and nearly demolished a rate-collector's house. In increasing fury and numbers they went to Earl Granville's collieries, stopped the engines, and ducked some of the men they found at work. In their madness they were merciless even to men of their own order. Potters too were turned out of the different manufactories where they were employed. The police office was attacked and the prisoners released. They fell on the Court of Requests at Shelton, destroying books and papers and furniture, and violently attacking the clerk. When they arrived at

*Cf. *The Life of Thomas Cooper (The Chartist)* written by himself (1886).

46

Arriving at the Swan Square in Burslem, they found another mob breaking into the George Inn. This place was forced, the cellars invaded, and drink again consumed to give a fiercer fury to those who had shared in it. These two mobs having united, were attacked by a number of soldiers, but only using the flat sides of their swords. This looked like a friendly warning on the part of the military — like the gleaming of teeth which could bite in case of need. There was also a troop of Dragoons from Newcastle, under the command of Major French, and these men were being drilled in "the Legs of Man" yard. Two hundred special constables were hiding, who, from all accounts, would have preferred to hide until the fray was over. Contemporary reports represent these poor specials as presenting anything but a valorous appearance, even though they were being primed with the best beer. Gathering contingents of desperate and curious men came from many quarters. Seeing this, Major Powys, who was a magistrate as well as a soldier, asked those who were quietly disposed to go home. He did this in Chapel Bank, and then in the market square. Finding this comparatively useless, he proceeded to read the Riot Act. This only produced a more menacing disposition to defy. He again appealed to the crowd to go home, but they stood before him in resolute defiance. Then came from his lips the ringing command, "Clear the streets!" Amid the rattling of swords drawn from their scabbards came the cry, "Charge!" The soldiers then drove in upon the mob, but again only used the flat sides of the swords. Confusion and noise prevailed everywhere, but the crowd driven away in one direction returned in another. Burslem market-place had many outlets, and these enabled the people to baffle somewhat the attacks of the soldiers. Some of these got separated in the roads, and were maltreated. This small success of the crowd fired them with greater daring, and sticks and stones were used with reckless courage. But above the uproar of this conflict in the market-place there came the piercing sounds from a band marching along Moorland Road. Soon there was a cry, "They are coming from Leek," and a wild shout of "Hooray." This movement led the soldiers to leave the market-place, and gallop towards the "Big House" at the Moorland Road entrance to the town. This new mob came on, composed of weavers from Leek, Congleton and Macclesfield. The poor wretches, from all accounts, did not present a very formidable aspect. They were mostly half-dressed and half-starved. The only really vigorous men among them were a few agricultural labourers whom they had picked up on the way. Many of them carried thick sticks and thin arms. Others mustered all the stones they could carry in torn aprons and handkerchiefs. They were a motley crew, pale-faced, and cadaverous looking. Near where they entered the town the special constables stood, and it is questionable which had the paler faces, the new crowd or these defenders of law and order. Major Powys demanded when he went out to these men what they wanted. The reply came quick, "Our rights and liberties, the Charter, and more to eat." Perhaps if this last want had been supplied by the wisdom of English statesmen and the more generous treatment of the employers, their rights and liberties, and the Charter, too, would have been sought in quieter and more loyal ways. "More to eat!" they cried, and who can say that their demand was unreasonable? It was the cry of divinely given appetites trampled upon by a false and wicked human policy, and when these two things come into collision, law and order, respectabilities, shams and pretences, without an element of justice, must go down or fight for ascendency. Major Powys, soldier-like, gave voice to the gibbering respectabilities when he said, "assembling in a disorderly mob is not the way to get your rights and liberties. I entreat you to disperse and go quietly to your homes." This advice was received with mocking and defiant yells. Major Powys did not tell these men how to get their rights and liberties. They had tried to get them by more orderly agitation for twelve years and failed. He told them to go quietly to their homes. But let it be remembered what many of those homes were. They were places robbed of nearly all the elements which make home. They were places where they saw the pinched faces of wives and children, and heard cries for food which they could not supply. To reason thus with these men was quite "proper" for a military magistrate, but it can be seen now that to take such advice would have been a miracle of self-restraint, and such miracles are not wrought by the grace of starvation.

49

"Rude comparisons you draw,
Words refuse to sate your maw,
Your gaunt limbs the cobweb law
　　Cannot hold.

You're not clogged with foolish pride,
But can seize a right denied,
Somehow God is on your side,
　　Hunger and cold."

That yell of defiance which rose from the crowd in response to Major Powys's words was not wholly of the devil's inspiration. Violence had been done to the rights and liberties of these men as wicked as the violence which was now provoked. "To destroy life and property" is as stupid as it is iniquitous, but let us recognise that it is equally stupid and iniquitous to provoke a destroying desperation. This had been done, cruelly and persistently done. Major Powys did not know that those he represented were primarily responsible for all the terrible possibilities which were before him in that awful hour. But the crowd knew this, and hence the loud mockery which followed his little preachment. This general yell was the signal for action. There went forth the cry, "We'll make the soldiers run and duck the specials behind." They were vain words, and they were followed by equally vain actions. Showers of stones were hurled at the soldiers, and the mob pressed forward, and those in front touched the horses' heads. It was now clearly seen that this seething mass of desperation must be resisted. Major Powys had shown remarkable restraint up to this ominous moment. Collision was now inevitable, and there went forth from his lips the fatal cry to his soldiers, "Fire!" Immediately the guns were raised, and the crowd shrank back instinctively, but vainly, owing to its own mass. "Food for powder" was plentiful and near at hand. The musketry rattled; but the rattle was soon drowned by cries of defiance and terror and agony from that writhing mass of human beings. Numbers fell to the ground, either wounded or forced down by the general rush which followed the firing of the muskets. The confusion was complete. Maddened and still desperate, the crowd broke and fled in different directions. Standing against the gate-post of the "Big House" was a young fellow from Leek, and it was said he had a stick in one hand and a stone in the other. It was also said on the very day of this riot that he was not taking part in it, but was one of those men whose curiosity will take a man to the very verge of peril. However this may be, the blood of the soldiers was up, and this youth's brains were blown out against the gate-post. He fell dead on the footpath, and military valour had secured one fatal trophy, such as it was. So many shots as were fired, though they did not find fatal lodgment in many cases, nevertheless wounded many, who were carried away by friends, or hobbled away themselves. Some, it is said, went away to die of their wounds, but their injuries were prudently concealed in this time of suspicion and terror. It was a miserable, hideous and loathsome conflict, but, thank God, the last of its kind which had darkened the Potteries so far in this country, and probably no other century will witness in our country an event so charged with tyranny and injustice, and with folly and wickedness . . ."

When I was a child, by an old potter (with an introduction by Robert Spence Watson) 1903.

17. The Great Durham Lock-Out, 1844

[*THE verses "The Miner's Complaint" were written by R. H. Fawcett, of South Wingate, and were published in "The Miners' Advocate" of 16th December, 1843. They were written during the attacks made on the colliers by Lord Londonderry. At this time miners were signed for a bond of eleven months. In April, 1844, the colliers refused to sign the bond and this caused the Great Durham Lock-out. The whole of the Durham and Northumberland coalfield was locked out and the miners were reduced to living in tents.*]

"THE MINER'S COMPLAINT"

"Alas! What will become of me,
What help for wife and family,
When work I cannot get?
Our bread is now become so small
Our children crying one and all
Oh, give a little bit!

How mournful such a tale to state,
Starvation seems to be my fate —
No food can we procure.
My tender wife exclaims, 'My dear,
I'll die for want of food, I fear;
Three days! Can I endure?'

Ah, this I cannot bear, dear wife.
Upon the road I'll venture life
And there I'll in an ambush lie:
And should a traveller appear
I'll cry, tho' trembling with fear,
'Your money or you die.'

'Speak not, my husband, thus,' she said
Then sighing faint, she dropped her head
And died — of HUNGER DIED!
My helpless babes, your mother's gone,
The spirit from starvation's flown,
From grief and sorrow's tide."

[*Ten more verses in like strain follow, in which the husband dies and the children are put into the Bastille — the workhouse. It ends:*]

"Rise, Britains, rise! Let despots know
That heaven will deal the avenging blow!
Out hearts too long have bled!"

PUNCH in July, 1844, made its own comment on the Durham dispute and on the Marquis of Londonderry, the colliery-owner, leading the attack on the miners:

"THE MARQUIS OF LONDONDERRY'S PITMEN. — There has been a great turn out of the Marquis of Londonderry's pitmen, for which incident, deny it as he may, we have little doubt that the marquis is uncommonly grateful, and for this reason; it affords him an opportunity for the exercise of his literary powers; and that the marquis is smitten with the fatal charms of pen, ink, and foolscap, who that has read the noble writer's histories and travels can deny; hence the marquis has, from Holderness House, sent to his pitmen several epistles full of 'paternal advice,' the result of this is the following answer of the pitmen to their anxious father, Londonderry."

DURHAM, JULY 22nd.

"MARQUIS, — We have received your letter that calls upon us to leave the union and return to our work. In answer to this we say, Oh marquis! leave you your union, that coals may be cheaper, and the pitmen's labour more abundant. You charge us with combining;

we, marquis, charge you with the like act; we combine with one another that we may have the value of the sweat of our brows; you belong to the coal trade union, to the union of masters, banded together to keep up the price of coals, to stint the supply of the market, that it may always bring a certain price. What, then, wealth may combine, but labour not? You conjure us to look upon the ruin we are bringing on our wives, our children, our county, and the country: we in reply, conjure you to consider the misery, the wretchedness, the suffering, that every winter is brought upon the London poor by the coal owners' union, that, obstinate for high prices, makes firing an unattainable luxury. You say that you will come among us, and proceed to eject us, taking especial care that the civil and military power shall be at hand, to support you. Oh father! is it thus you will show your paternal love to your pitmen's little ones? Come among us, marquis, pray come, and never dream that we shall want the civil and military power to settle the differences between us. No, fear not, after a little talk, we shall agree in amity and love; and in the hope of this dear father, we remain your affectionate children of the pit."

PUNCH, *July, 1844*

18. The Blackleg Miners

[*IN THE Durham lock-out, blacklegs were stripped of their clothing and tools, which were then thrown down the pit-shaft. Typical of the miners' militant attitude to the non-unionist is the ballad "The Blackleg Miners" probably dating to the 1840s:*]

Oh, early in the evening, just after dark,
The blackleg miners creep out and go to work,
With their moleskin trousers and dirty old shirt
Go the dirty blackleg miners!

They take their picks and down they go,
To dig out the coal tha's lying down below,
And there isn't a woman in this town row
Will look at a blackleg miner!

Oh, Delaval is a terrible place,
They rub wet clay in the blackleg's face,
And round the pit-heaps they run a foot-race
With the dirty blackleg miners!

Oh, don't go near the Seghill mine,
For across the mainway they hang a line,
To catch the throat and break the spine
Of the dirty blackleg miners!

They'll take your tools and your duds as well,
And throw them down in the pit of hell,
Its down you go and fare you well,
You dirty blackleg miners!

So join the union while you may
Don't you wait till your dying day
For that may not be far away,
You dirty blackleg miners!

19. The Engineers' Strike and Lock-Out, 1851-2

"PRIOR to the year 1850 each of the several branches of the engineering trade had their own separate and independent union. The practice of systematic overtime had so extended in this trade that the workmen in the various branches became very dissatisfied with the practice, and determined, if possible, to put a stop to it. In addition to which, piecework was also extensively resorted to, and this practice was condemned as an innovation injurious to the workmen. These questions, and especially overtime, had engaged the attention of the engineering trades for many years; so far back as 1836 a compromise had been arranged in London as to overtime, which was thereafter to be paid for at an additional rate. The compromise, in so far as London was concerned, seems to have been adhered to, and extra pay was made for overtime. In Lancashire, however, no such general rule existed, and, consequently, disputes were frequent, and strikes often occurred. Indeed, the matters were so often in dispute that strikes, on a small scale, became chronic in the Lancashire district. At last it was determined to deal with the whole matter, and to settle the question once for all.

In September, 1850, a delegate meeting, or conference of the several branches of the engineering trades, consisting of machinists, millwrights, smiths, patternmakers, &c., was held in Birmingham, when the questions of overtime and piecework were discussed, and a plan of action agreed upon. The most important result of the agitation was the amalgamation of the several small or local unions into one solid body, henceforth to be known as the "Amalgamated Society of Engineers" . . . The movement in favour of a general union of all the branches of the trade, and their consolidation into one society, was so popular that by the end of 1851 the union had 121 branches in various parts of the country, the total membership being 11,829 members. Its income in that year was £22,807 8s. 8d.; its expenditure, £13,325; and its total available balance in hand, £22,000. This great expansion and success led the Lancashire delegates to declare "that they were now strong enough to act effectually," a statement concurred in by the members.

The Amalgamated Society of Engineers had from the hour of its birth been pledged to an attempt to abolish systematic overtime and piecework in the iron trades. But the Council of the union did not take any step to give effect to the resolve until July 1851, when a circular was issued to the whole of the members with the view of ascertaining their opinions as to immediate action, and if so in what direction. Out of the 11,829 members 9,000 voted, and of these only sixteen declared in favour of overtime and piecework. With so overwhelming an opinion in favour of the abolition of these practices, the Council addressed a circular to the masters intimating that overtime and piecework were to cease from and after December 31st, 1851, except in cases of necessity, when, if overtime was resorted to, it must be paid for at the rate of double time. The language and tone of this circular were moderate and conciliatory throughout.

This circular was regarded as an ultimatum, and was accepted by the employers as a declaration of war. An Employers' Association was formed to resist the demands of the workmen, and, as eventually was proved, to try and crush the union. Before the issue of the circular matters became a little complicated by the dispute at Oldham between Messrs. Hibbert and Platt and their workmen, respecting overtime and the employment of labourers in working machines, which the members of the union thought ought only to be worked by mechanics. After some negotiation, the firm consented to a compromise, which the Council of the society regarded as fair; the men refused to acquiesce, and struck, but the Council refused strike pay, and the men returned to work on the condition that the employment of labourers should cease at Christmas, 1851. As the men had determined to strike if the conditions were not adhered to, the masters met after the receipt of the circular and determined to close their establishments should a strike take place.

On January 1st, 1852, the men left their work at the end of the regular day's work of ten hours; and on the 10th the masters closed their establishments, thus making it a lockout instead of a strike. About 15,000 men appear to have been locked out on this occasion. On January 24th the masters issued their declaration to the effect that their establishments would reopen in February to all workmen who would sign the declaration, or document, renouncing the union. Some men returned to work, and after struggling on till the end of March, the society virtually gave up the contest. On March 30th the Manchester District Committee memorialised the masters to withdraw the declaration, stating their willingness to withdraw the circulars of October 2nd and November 24th, 1851; but the masters refused to treat, and stood by the "declaration." By the end of April the men had returned to work, having signed the declaration to leave the union. The sequel shows that this enforced declaration failed of its intended object, the break-up of the union.

The net cost of the strike and lockout, to the Amalgamated Society, was £35,459 0s. 9d.; but the expenditure largely exceeded that sum, as the total amount paid as donation to men out of work in 1851-52 amounted to £48,670, besides which a large amount was subscribed by other trades, the total being £4,899 15s. 6d.; and by private persons £4,034 7s. 3d. The two latter sums were distributed mainly to non-union men locked out by the employers. The total loss of members through the lockout and consequent signing of the declaration was 2,092; but the society recovered over one-half in the following year, and by the end of 1854 the total number of members was equal to that before the lockout. A number of men, rather than sign the declaration, emigrated to the Colonies and to America. This led to branches being formed, many of which have grown to be healthy branches of the parent society. It is stated that the funds for emigration were mostly advanced by private persons — one gentleman lent £1,000 for the purpose, on their simple bond. All the money so advanced was repaid, with interest.

The object sought by the society was not attained, and much suffering was experienced during the contest; but the institution of the Amalgamated Society of Engineers was worth all the expenditure, for it has grown to be the most powerful and useful association of modern times. The society keeps its own poor, sustains its own sick, buries in decency its own deceased members and their wives, and maintains for its members a rate of wages which could not otherwise have been obtained and continued in this country."

GEORGE HOWELL, Great Strikes: Their Origin,
Cost and Results (*C.W.S. Annual 1889*)

20. The Preston Spinners' Strike, 1853-4

DICKENS AS STRIKE REPORTER

[*AT PRESTON, in 1853, spinners at certain factories struck for more wages and the employers replied with a general lock-out. Blacklegs were imported and the strike leaders arrested. Finally, the men were driven back to work and their leaders released without trial.*]

ON STRIKE
[FEBRUARY 11, 1854]

"Travelling down to Preston a week from this date, I chanced to sit opposite to a very acute, very determined, very emphatic personage, with a stout railway rug so drawn over his chest that he looked as if he were sitting up in bed with his great-coat, hat, and gloves on, severely contemplating your humble servant from behind a large blue and grey checked counterpane. In calling him emphatic, I do not mean that he was warm; he was coldly and bitingly emphatic as a frosty wind is.

'You are going through to Preston, sir?' says he, as soon as we were clear of the Primrose Hill tunnel.

The receipt of his question was like the receipt of a jerk of the nose; he was so short and sharp.

'Yes.'

'This Preston strike is a nice piece of business!' said the gentleman. 'A pretty piece of business!'

'It is very much to be deplored,' said I, 'on all accounts.'

'They want to be ground. That's what they want, to bring 'em to their senses,' said the gentleman; whom I had already began to call in my own mind Mr. Snapper, and whom I may as well call by that name here as by any other.

I deferentially enquired, who wanted to be ground?

'The hands,' said Mr. Snapper. 'The hands on strike, and the hands who help 'em.'

I remarked that if that was all they wanted, they must be a very unreasonable people, for surely they had had a little grinding, one way and another, already. Mr. Snapper eyed me with sternness, and after opening and shutting his leathern-gloved hands several times outside his counterpane, asked me abruptly, 'Was I a delegate?

I set Mr. Snapper right on that point, and told him I was no delegate.

'I am glad to hear it,' said Mr. Snapper. 'But a friend to the Strike, I believe?'

'Not at all,' said I.

'A friend to the Lock-out?' pursued Mr. Snapper.

'Not in the least,' said I.

Mr. Snapper's rising opinion of me fell again, and he gave me to understand that a man *must* either be a friend to the Masters or a friend to the Hands.

'He may be a friend to both,' said I.

Mr. Snapper didn't see that; there was no medium in the Political Economy of the subject. I retorted on Mr. Snapper, that Political Economy was a great and useful science in its own way and its own place; but that I did not transplant my definition of it from the Common Prayer Book, and make it a great king above all gods. Mr. Snapper tucked himself up as if to keep me off, folded his arms on the top of his counterpane, leaned back, and looked out of window.

'Pray what would you have, sir,' enquired Mr. Snapper, suddenly withdrawing his eyes from the prospect to me, 'in the relations between Capital and Labour, *but* Political Economy?'

I always avoid the stereotyped terms in these discussions as much as I can, for I have observed, in my little way, that they often supply the place of sense and moderation. I therefore took my gentleman up with the words employers and employed, in preference to Capital and Labour.

'I believe,' said I, 'that into the relations between employers and employed, as into all the relations of this life, there must enter something of feeling and sentiment; something of mutual explana-

61

tion, forbearance, and consideration; something which is not to be found in Mr. M'Culloch's dictionary, and is not exactly stateable in figures; otherwise those relations are wrong and rotten at the core and will never bear sound fruit.'

Mr. Snapper laughed at me. As I thought I had just as good reason to laugh at Mr. Snapper, I did so, and we were both contented.

'Ah!' said Mr. Snapper, patting his counterpane with a hard touch. 'You know very little of the improvident and unreasoning habits of the common people, *I* see.'

'Yet I know something of those people, too,' was my reply. 'In fact, Mr. —,' I had so nearly called him Snapper! 'in fact, sir, I doubt the existence at this present time of many faults that are merely class faults. In the main, I am disposed to think that whatever faults you may find to exist, in your own neighbourhood for instance, among the hands, you will find tolerably equal in amount among the masters also, and even among the classes above the masters. They will be modified by circumstances, and they will be the less excusable among the better-educated, but they will be pretty fairly distributed. I have a strong expectation that we shall live to see the conventional adjectives now apparently inseparable from the phrases working people and lower orders, gradually fall into complete disuse for this reason.'

'Well, but we began with strikes,' Mr. Snapper observed impatiently. 'The masters have never had any share in strikes.'

'Yet I have heard of strikes once upon a time in that same county of Lancashire,' said I, 'which were not disagreeable to some masters when they wanted a pretext for raising prices.'

'Do you mean to say those masters had any hand in getting up those strikes?' asked Mr. Snapper.

'You will perhaps obtain better information among persons engaged in some Manchester branch trades, who have good memories,' said I.

Mr. Snapper had no doubt, after this, that I thought the hands had a right to combine?

'Surely,' said I. 'A perfect right to combine in any lawful manner. The fact of their being able to combine and accustomed to combine may, I can easily conceive, be a protection to them. The blame even of this business is not all on one side. I think the associated Lock-out was a grave error. And when you Preston masters—'

'*I* am not a Preston master,' interrupted Mr. Snapper.

'When the respectable combined body of Preston masters,' said I, 'in the beginning of this unhappy difference, laid down the principle that no man should be employed henceforth who belonged to any combination — such as their own — they attempted to carry with a high hand a partial and unfair impossibility, and were obliged to abandon it. This was an unwise proceeding and the first defeat.'

Mr. Snapper had known, all along, that I was no friend to the masters.

'Pardon me,' said I, 'I am unfeignedly a friend to the masters, and have many friends among them.'

'Yet you think these hands in the right?' quoth Mr. Snapper.

'By no means,' said I; 'I fear they are at present engaged in an unreasonable struggle, wherein they began ill and cannot end well.'

Mr. Snapper, evidently regarding me as neither fish, flesh, nor fowl, begged to know after a pause if he might enquire whether I was going to Preston on business?

Indeed I was going there, in my unbusinesslike manner, I confessed, to look at the strike.

'To look at the strike!' echoed Mr. Snapper, fixing his hat on firmly with both hands. 'To look at it! Might I ask you now, with what object you are going to look at it?'

'Certainly,' said I, 'I read, even in liberal pages, the hardest Political Economy — of an extraordinary description too sometimes, and certainly not to be found in the books — as the only touchstone of this strike. I see, this very day, in a to-morrow's liberal paper, some astonishing novelties in the politico-economical way, showing how profits and wages have no connexion whatever;

coupled with such references to these hands as might be made by a very irascible General to rebels and brigands in arms. Now, if it be the case that some of the highest virtues of the working people still shine through them brighter than ever in their conduct of this mistake of theirs, perhaps the fact may reasonably suggest to me — and to others besides me — that there is some little thing wanting in the relations between them and their employers, which neither political economy nor Drum-head proclamation writing will altogether supply, and which we cannot too soon or too temperately unite in trying to find out.'

Mr. Snapper after again opening and shutting his gloved hands several times, drew the counterpane higher over his chest, and went to bed in disgust. He got up at Rugby, took himself and counterpane into another carriage, and left me to pursue my journey alone.

When I got to Preston, it was four o'clock in the afternoon. The day being Saturday and market-day, a foreigner might have expected, from among so many idle and not over-fed people as the town contained, to find a turbulent, ill-conditioned crowd in the streets. But, except for the cold smokeless factory chimneys, the placards at the street corners, and the groups of working people attentively reading them, nor foreigner nor Englishman could have had the least suspicion that there existed any interruption to the usual labours of the place. The placards thus perused were not remarkable for their logic certainly, and did not make the case particularly clear; but, considering that they emanated from, and were addressed to, people who had been out of employment for three-and-twenty consecutive weeks, at least they had little passion in them, though they had not much reason. Take the worst I could find:

'FRIENDS AND FELLOW OPERATIVES,
    'Accept the grateful thanks of twenty thousand struggling Operatives, for the help you have showered upon Preston since the present contest commenced.

64

'Your kindness and generosity, your patience and long-continued support deserve every praise, and are only equalled by the heroic and determined perseverance of the outraged and insulted factory workers of Preston, who have been struggling for some months, and are, at this inclement season of the year, bravely battling for the rights of themselves and the whole toiling community.

'For many years before the strike took place at Preston, the Operatives were the down trodden and insulted serfs of their Employers, who in times of good trade and general prosperity, wrung from their labour a California of gold, which is now being used to crush those who created it, still lower and lower in the scale of civilisation. This has been the result of our commercial prosperity! – *more wealth for the rich and more poverty for the Poor!* Because the workpeople of Preston protested against this state of things – because they combined in a fair and legitimate way for the purpose of getting a reasonable share of the reward of their own labour, the *fair dealing* Employers of Preston, to their eternal shame and disgrace, *locked up* their Mills, and at one fell swoop deprived, as they thought, from twenty to thirty thousand human beings of the means of existence. Cruelty and tyranny always defeat their own object; it was so in this case, and to the honour and credit of the working classes of this country, we have to record, that, those whom the rich and wealthy sought to destroy, the poor and industrious have protected from harm. This love of justice and hatred of wrong, is a noble feature in the character and disposition of the working man, and gives us hope that in the future, this world will become what its great architect intended, not a place of sorrow, toil, oppression and wrong, but the dwelling place and the abode of peace, plenty, happiness and love, where avarice and all the evil passions engendered by the present system of fraud and injustice shall not have a place.

'The earth was not made for the misery of its people; intellect was not given to man to make himself and fellow creatures un-happy. No, the fruitfulness of the soil and the wonderful inven-tions – the result of mind – all proclaim that these things were bestowed upon us for our happiness and well-being, and not for the misery and degradation of the human race.

'It may serve the manufacturers and all who run away with the lion's share of labour's produce, to say that the *impartial* God intended that there should be a *partial* distribution of his blessings. But we know that it is against nature to believe, that those who plant and reap all the grain, should not have enough to make a mess of porridge; and we know that those who weave all the cloth should not want a yard to cover their persons, whilst those who never wove an inch have more calico, silks and satins, than would serve the reasonable wants of a dozen working men and their families.

'This system of giving everything to the few, and nothing to the many, has lasted long enough and we call upon the working people of this country to be determined to establish a new and improved system — a system that shall give to all who labour, a fair share of those blessings and comforts which their toil produce; in short, we wish to see that divine precept enforced, which says, "Those who will not work, shall not eat."

'The task is before you, working men; if you think the good which would result from its accomplishment, is worth struggling for, set to work and cease not, until you have obtained the *good time coming,* not only for the Preston Operatives, but for yourselves as well.

                                    '*By Order of the Committee.*
'MURPHY'S TEMPERANCE HOTEL, CHAPEL WALKS,
     'PRESTON, *January* 24th, 1854.'

It is a melancholy thing that it should not occur to the Committee to consider what would become of themselves, their friends, and fellow operatives, if those calicoes, silks, and satins, were *not* worn in very large quantities; but I shall not enter into that question. As I had told my friend Snapper, what I wanted to see with my own eyes, was, how these people acted under a mistaken impression, and what qualities they showed, even at that disadvantage, which ought to be the strength and peace — not the

66

weakness and trouble — of the community. I found, even from this literature, however, that all masters were not indiscriminately unpopular. Witness the following verses from the New Song of the Preston Strike:

'There's Henry Hornby, of Blackburn, he is a jolly brick,
He fits the Preston masters nobly, and is very bad to trick;
He pays his hands a good price, and I hope he will never sever,
So we'll sing success to Hornby, and Blackburn for ever.

'There is another gentleman, I'm sure you'll all lament,
In Blackburn for him they're raising a monument,
You know his name, 'tis of great fame, it was late Eccles of
   honour,
May Hopwood, and Sparrow, and Hornby live for ever.

'So now it is time to finish and end my rhyme,
We warn these Preston Cotton Lords to mind for future time.
With peace and order too I hope we shall be clever,
We sing success to Stockport and Blackburn for ever.
         Now, lads, give your minds to it.'

The balance sheet of the receipts and expenditure for the twenty-third week of the strike was extensively posted. The income for that week was two thousand one hundred and forty pounds odd. Some of the contributors were poetical. As,

'Love to all and peace to the dead,
May the poor now in need never want bread —

three-and-sixpence.' The following poetical remonstrance was appended to the list of contributions from the Gorton district:

'Within these walls the lasses fair
Refuse to contribute their share,
Careless of duty — blind to fame,
For shame, ye lasses, oh! for shame!
Come, pay up, lasses, think what's right,
Defend your trade with all your might;

For if you don't the world will blame,
And cry, ye lasses, oh, for shame!
Let's hope in future all will pay,
That Preston folks may shortly say —
That by your aid they have obtain'd
The greatest victory ever gained.'

Some of the subscribers veiled their names under encouraging sentiments, as Not tired yet, All in a mind, Win the day, Fraternity, and the like. Some took jocose appellations, as A stunning friend, Two to one Preston wins, Nibbling Joe, and The Donkey Driver. Some expressed themselves through their trades, as Cobbler Dick, sixpence, The tailor true, sixpence, Shoemaker, a shilling, The chirping blacksmith, sixpence, and A few of Maskery's most feeling coachmakers, three-and-threepence. An old balance sheet for the fourteenth week of the Strike was headed with this quotation from Mr. Carlyle, 'Adversity is sometimes hard upon a man; but for one man who can stand prosperity, there are a hundred that will stand adversity.' The Elton district prefaced its report with these lines:

'Oh! ye who start a noble scheme,
    For general good designed;
Ye workers in a cause that tends
    To benefit your kind!
Mark out the path ye fain would tread,
    The game ye mean to play;
And if it be an honest one,
    Keep steadfast in your way!

'Although you may not gain at once
    The points ye most desire;
Be patient — time can wonders work;
    Plod on, and do not tire;
Obstructions, too, may crowd your path,
    In threatening, stern array;
Yet flinch not! fear not! they may prove
    Mere shadows in your way.

'Then, while there's work for you to do,
    Stand not despairing by,
Let "forward" be the move ye make,
    Let "onward" be your cry;
And when success has crowned your plans,
    'Twill all your pains repay,
To see the good your labour's done –
    Then droop not on your way.'

In this list, 'Bear ye one another's burthens,' sent one Pound fifteen. 'We'll stand to our text, see that ye love one another,' sent nineteen shillings. 'Christopher Hardman's men again, they say they can always spare one shilling out of ten,' sent two-and-sixpence. The following masked threats were the worst feature in any bill I saw:—

'If that fiddler at Uncle Tom's Cabin blowing room does not pay, Punch will set his legs straight.

'If that drawer at card side and those two slubbers do not pay, Punch will say something about their bustles.

'If that winder at last shift does not pay next week, Punch will tell about her actions.'

But, on looking at this bill again, I found that it came from Bury and related to Bury, and had nothing to do with Preston. The Masters' placards were not torn down or disfigured, but were being read quite as attentively as those on the opposite side.

That evening, the Delegates from the surrounding districts were coming in, according to custom, with their subscription lists for the week just closed. These delegates meet on Sunday as their only day of leisure; when they have made their reports, they go back to their homes and their Monday's work. On Sunday morning, I repaired to the Delegates' meeting.

These assemblages take place in a cockpit, which, in the better times of our fallen land, belonged to the late Lord Derby for the purposes of the intellectual recreation implied in its name. I was directed to the cockpit up a narrow lane, tolerably crowded by the lower sort of working people. Personally, I was quite unknown in the town, but every one made way for me to pass, with great civility, and perfect good humour. Arrived at the cockpit door, and expressing my desire to see and hear, I was handed through the crowd, down into the pit, and up again, until I found myself seated on the topmost circular bench, within one of the secretary's table, and within three of the chairman. Behind the chairman was a great crown on the top of a pole, made of part-coloured calico, and strongly suggestive of May-day. There was no other symbol or ornament in the place.

It was hotter than any mill or factory I have ever been in; but there was a stove down in the sanded pit, and delegates were seated close to it, and one particular delegate often warmed his hands at it, as if he were chilly. The air was so intensely close and hot, that at first I had but a confused perception of the delegates down in the pit, and the dense crowd of eagerly listening men and women (but not very many of the latter) filling all the benches and choking such narrow standing room as there was. When the atmosphere cleared a little on better acquaintance, I found the question under discussion to be, Whether the Manchester Delegates in attendance from the Labour Parliament, should be heard?

If the Assembly, in respect of quietness and order, were put in comparison with the House of Commons, the Right Honourable the Speaker himself would decide for Preston. The chairman was a Preston weaver, two or three and fifty years of age, perhaps; a man with a capacious head, rather long dark hair growing at the sides and back, a placid attentive face, keen eyes, a particularly composed manner, a quiet voice, and a persuasive action of his right arm. Now look'ee heer my friends. See what t' question is. T' question is, sholl these heer men be heerd. Then 't cooms to this, what ha' these men got t' tell us? Do they bring mooney? If they bring mooney t'ords t' expences o' this strike, they're welcome. For, Brass, my friends, is what we want, and what we must ha' (hear hear hear!). Do they coom to us wi' any suggestion for the conduct of this strike? If they do, they're welcome. Let

70

'em give us their advice and we will hearken to 't. But, if these men coom heer, to tell us what t' Labour Parliament is, or what Ernest Jones's opinion is, or t' bring in politics and differences amoong us when what we want is 'armony, brotherly love, and con-cord; then I say t' you, decide for yoursel' carefully, whether these men ote to be heerd in this place. (Hear hear hear! and No no no!) Chairman sits down, earnestly regarding delegates, and holding both arms of his chair. Looks extremely sensible; his plain coarse working man's shirt collar easily turned down over his loose Belcher neckerchief. Delegate who has moved that Manchester delegates be heard, presses motion – Mr. Chairman, will that delegate tell us, as a man, that these men have anything to say concerning this present strike and lock-out, for we have a deal of business to do, and what concerns this present strike and lock-out is our business and nothing else is. (Hear hear hear!) – Delegate in question will not compromise the fact; these men want to defend the Labour Parliament from certain charges made against them. – Very well, Mr. Chairman, Then I move as an amendment that you do not hear these men now, and that you proceed wi' business – and if you don't I'll look after you, I tell you that. (Cheers and laughter) – Coom lads, prove't then! – Two or three hands for the delegates; all the rest for the business. Motion lost, amendment carried, Manchester deputation not to be heard.

But now, starts up the delegate from Throstletown, in a dreadful state of mind. Mr. Chairman, I hold in my hand a bill; a bill that requires and demands explanation from you, sir; an offensive bill; a bill posted in my town of Throstletown without my knowledge, without the knowledge of my fellow delegates who are here beside me; a bill purporting to be posted by the authority of the massed committee, sir, and of which my fellow delegates and myself were kept in ignorance. Why are we to be slighted? Why are we to be insulted? Why are we to be meanly stabbed in the dark? Why *is* this assassin-like course of conduct to be pursued towards us? Why is Throstletown, which has nobly assisted you, the operatives of Preston, in this great struggle, and which has brought its contribution up to the full sevenpence a loom, to be thus degraded, thus aspersed, thus traduced, thus despised, thus outraged in its feelings by un-English and unmanly conduct? Sir, I hand you up that bill, and I require of you, sir, to give me a satisfactory explanation of that bill. And I have that confidence in your known integrity, sir, as to be sure that you will give it, and that you will tell us who is to blame, and that you will make reparation to Throstletown for this scandalous treatment. Then, in hot blood, up starts Gruffshaw (professional speaker) who is somehow responsible for this bill. O my friends, but explanation is required here! O my friends, but it is fit and right that you should have the dark ways of the real traducers and apostates, and the real un-English stabbers, laid bare before you. My friends when this dark conspiracy first began — But here the persuasive right hand of the chairman falls gently on Gruffshaw's shoulder. Gruffshaw stops in full boil. My friends, these are hard words of my friend Gruffshaw, and this is not the business — No more it is, and once again, sir, I, the delegate who said I would look after you, do move that you proceed to business! — Preston has not the strong relish for personal altercation that Westminster hath. Motion seconded and carried, business passed to, Gruffshaw dumb.

Perhaps the world could not afford a more remarkable contrast than between the deliberate collected manner of these men proceeding with their business, and the clash and hurry of the engines among which their lives are passed. Their astonishing fortitude and perseverance; their high sense of honour among themselves; the extent to which they are impressed with the responsibility that is upon them of setting a careful example, and keeping their order out of any harm and loss of reputation; the noble readiness in them to help one another, of which most medical practitioners and working clergymen can give so many affecting examples; could scarcely ever be plainer to an ordinary observer of human nature than in this cockpit. To hold, for a minute, that the great mass of them were not sincerely actuated by the belief that all these qualities were bound up in what they were doing, and that they were doing right, seemed to me little short of an impossibility. As the different delegates (some in the very dress in which they had

72

left the mill last night) reported the amounts sent from the various places they represented, this strong faith on their parts seemed expressed in every tone and every look that was capable of expressing it. One man was raised to enthusiasm by his pride in bringing so much; another man was ashamed and depressed because he brought so little; this man triumphantly made it known that he could give you, from the store in hand, a hundred pounds in addition next week, if you should want it; and that man pleaded that he hoped his district would do better before long; but I could as soon have doubted the existence of the walls that enclosed us, as the earnestness with which they spoke (many of them referring to the children who were to be born to labour after them) of 'this great, this noble, gallant, godlike struggle.' Some designing and turbulent spirits among them, no doubt there are; but I left the place with a profound conviction that their mistake is generally an honest one, and that it is sustained by the good that is in them and not by the evil.

Neither by night nor by day was there any interruption to the peace of the streets. Nor was this an accidental state of things, for the police records of the town are eloquent to the same effect. I traversed the streets very much, and was, as a stranger, the subject of a little curiosity among the idlers; but I met with no rudeness or ill-temper. More than once, when I was looking at the printed balance-sheets to which I have referred, and could not quite comprehend the setting forth of the figures, a bystander of the working class interposed with his explanatory forefinger and helped me out. Although the pressure in the cockpit on Sunday was excessive, and the heat of the room obliged me to make my way out as I best could before the close of the proceedings, none of the people whom I put to inconvenience showed the least impatience; all helped me, and all cheerfully acknowledged my word of apology as I passed. It is very probably, notwithstanding, that they may have supposed from my being there at all — I and my companion were the only persons present, not of their own order — that I was there to carry what I heard and saw to the opposite side; indeed one speaker seemed to intimate as much.

On the Monday at noon, I returned to this cockpit, to see the people paid. It was then about half filled, principally with girls and women. They were all seated, waiting, with nothing to occupy their attention; and were just in that state when the unexpected appearance of a stranger differently dressed from themselves, and with his own individual peculiarities of course, might, without offence, have had something droll in it even to more polite assemblies. But I stood there, looking on, as free from remarks as if I had come to be paid with the rest. In the place which the secretary had occupied yesterday, stood a dirty little common table, covered with five-penny piles of halfpence. Before the paying began, I wondered who was going to receive these very small sums; but when it did begin, the mystery was soon cleared up. Each of these piles was the change for sixpence, deducting a penny. All who were paid, in filing round the building to prevent confusion, had to pass this table on the way out; and the greater part of the unmarried girls stopped here, to change, each a sixpence, and subscribe her weekly penny in aid of the people on strike who had families. A very large majority of these girls and women were comfortably dressed in all respects, clean, wholesome and pleasant-looking. There was a prevalent neatness and cheerfulness, and an almost ludicrous absence of anything like sullen discontent.

Exactly the same appearances were observable on the same day, at a not numerously attended open air meeting in 'Chadwick's Orchard' — which blossoms in nothing but red bricks. Here, the chairman of yesterday presided in a cart, from which speeches were delivered. The proceedings commenced with the following sufficiently general and discursive hymn, given out by a workman from Burnley, and sung in long metre by the whole audience:

'Assembled beneath thy broad blue sky,
To thee, O God, thy children cry,
Thy needy creatures on Thee call,
For thou art great and good to all.

'Thy bounty smiles on every side,
And no good thing hast thou denied;
But men of wealth and men of power,
Like locusts, all our gifts devour.

'Awake, ye sons of toil! nor sleep
While millions starve, while millions weep;
Demand your rights; let tyrants see
You are resolved that you'll be free.'

Mr. Hollins's Sovereign Mill was open all this time. It is a very beautiful mill, containing a large amount of valuable machinery, to which some recent ingenious improvements have been added. Four hundred people could find employment in it; there were eighty-five at work, of whom five had 'come in' that morning. They looked, among the vast array of motionless power-looms, like a few remaining leaves in a wintry forest. They were protected by the police (very prudently not obtruded on the scenes I have described), and were stared at every day when they came out, by a crowd which had never been large in reference to the numbers on strike, and had diminished to a score or two. One policeman at the door sufficed to keep order then. These eighty-five were people of exceedingly decent appearance, chiefly women, and were evidently not in the least uneasy for themselves. I heard of one girl among them, and only one, who had been hustled and struck in a dark street.

In any aspect in which it can be viewed, this strike and lock-out is a deplorable calamity. In its waste of time, in its waste of a great people's energy, in its waste of wages, in its waste of wealth that seeks to be employed, in its encroachment on the means of many thousands who are labouring from day to day, in the gulf of separation it hourly deepens between those whose interests must be understood to be identical or must be destroyed, it is a great national affliction. But, at this pass, anger is of no use, starving out is of no use — for what will that do, five years hence, but overshadow all the mills in England with the growth of a bitter remembrance? — political economy is a mere skeleton unless it has a little human covering and filling out, a little human bloom upon it, and a little human warmth in it. Gentlemen are found, in great manufacturing towns, ready enough to extol imbecile mediation with dangerous madmen abroad; can none of them be brought to think of authorised mediation and explanation at home? I do not suppose that such a knotted difficulty as this, is to be at all untangled by a morning-party in the Adelphi; but I would entreat both sides now so miserably opposed, to consider whether there are no men in England, above suspicion, to whom they might refer the matters in dispute, with a perfect confidence above all things in the desire of those men to act justly, and in their sincere attachment to their countrymen of every rank and to their country. Masters right, or men right; masters wrong, or men wrong; both right, or both wrong; there is certain ruin to both in the continuance of frequent revival of this breach. And from the ever-widening circle of their decay, what drop in the social ocean shall be free!"

CHARLES DICKENS, *Miscellaneous Papers*
(1854)

21. Northampton Boot and Shoe Makers, 1857-9

"THIS strike arose from an attempt to prevent the introduction of machinery into the manufacture of boots and shoes. Various attempts had been made to apply machinery to this trade, and in 1857 the sewing machine for "closing" the "uppers" was introduced. No serious resistance was offered to the use of the sewing machine in London, in the large towns of the North, or in the South and West of England, by the workmen engaged in the boot and shoe trades. But in the Midland towns — Northampton, Stafford, Daventry, Kettering, Towcester, and Wellingborough — an organised resistance was determined upon. The first of these new machines seems to have been brought to Northampton in November, 1857. Alarm and excitement rapidly spread, and an open-air meeting was forthwith convened, which was attended by large numbers, when it was declared that ruin was threatened to the entire trade, by loss of employment, lower wages, and other evils consequent thereupon. A second meeting was held a few days later at the Milton Hall, in Northampton, at which meeting the operatives practically committed themselves to resistance if sewing machines were introduced into the trade.

At the first meeting a deputation was appointed to wait upon the employers with respect to the employment of the new sewing machines, when many of the masters declared that they were unfavourable to their use, and would not adopt them, unless driven thereto by the competition of other masters. This interview seems to have encouraged the men to open resistance. On November 11th the operatives passed a resolution declaring their determination not to "make up" any work for any employer who introduced machine-prepared tops. The men in two shops where these "closed uppers" were being used were at once called out. Nearly all the operatives complied with the order, as did also those employed in a third shop, where similar closed uppers were soon after given out. But a few old hands refused to join in the strike, and these were speedily reinforced by a number of fresh hands drawn from the neighbouring villages, under an offer of increased wages.

During December, 1857, and January and February, 1858, meetings were held in the neighbouring towns and villages, and subscriptions were solicited for the support of those on strike. But, although the sympathies of nearly the entire body of the operatives appeared to be in favour of resistance, judging from the meetings held, and the resolutions passed thereat, the funds subscribed were not adequate for the support of those on strike, nor were they in proportion to the apparent enthusiasm evoked. During these three winter months many of the men obtained work elsewhere, so that very little distress was experienced at that period. As no general union existed at this time amongst the operatives, a movement was inaugurated to institute a union. In April, 1858, the Northamptonshire Boot and Shoe Makers' Mutual Protection Society was established, one of the objects of which was, as stated in the rules, to prevent the introduction of machinery into the trade. The great majority of the men hastened to join the new society, but still the number of hands who continued at work was nearly sufficient for the firms whose workmen were on strike, and machine-made tops were made up for the masters elsewhere.

Considerable feeling was evoked in April and May, 1858, against the firms engaged in the strike, and the workpeople who continued in their employ. Several cases of intimidation were brought before the justices, but no serious case of violence seems to have occurred.

For some time the strike was confined to the question of machinery, but the Kettering branch of the union complicated the matter by a new rule against apprentices; this weakened the union. The strike continued without success until October, 1858, when it was resolved to extend the strike against all employers who gave work to those who continued to work for the firms struck against after the 16th of that month. The names of the obnoxious persons were printed and circulated. Shortly after this, a shop in Kettering gave notice of a reduction in the price of making up some descriptions of shoes. The men determined to resist the reduction and struck. The general union refused to support them, or were unable to give strike pay. The Kettering branch thereupon seceded, and the general body became weakened and dissatisfied.

The strike continued until February, 1859, when all the leading houses in Northampton, Stafford, and other places gave notice of their determination to introduce machines, and twenty of the principal shops in Northampton agreed to use machine-made uppers, while seventeen of the employers of Stafford pledged themselves not to employ any fresh hands from Northampton if the men resisted. A general strike was then determined upon. About 1,500 men left the town of Northampton, and went on tramp seeking employment; but many of those who at first joined in the strike returned to their work after two or three weeks. The strike did not on the whole commend itself to the operatives in other towns, nor to the workmen in other trades, so that most of those who left Northampton subsequently returned, to find their places filled with other hands. Much distress was in consequence experienced by those who had engaged in the general strike. Funds were subscribed by various trade societies, in London and elsewhere, but most of the money was expended in providing means for those on tramp; very little was left for the families at home. The strike was finally ended by the employers offering and the men accepting a slight advance in prices for "making up machine-prepared tops." This struggle lasted about eighteen months. No estimate of the losses incurred, or of the actual cost, can be obtained; but it was costly and disastrous to all concerned in all respects."

GEORGE HOWELL, Great Strikes: Their Origin,
Cost and Results (*C.W.S. Annual* 1889)

22. Builders' Strike and Lock-Out, 1859-60: The Nine-Hours Movement

"DURING the latter part of the year the chief masters and the men in the building trades of London were in a state of open war. The masters closed their establishments on August 6th, and afterwards only employed men who would sign a document. The men refused, to the number it was said of 20,000. The Conference of the trades' societies distributed certain sums among their members; and in the sixth week as many as 14,000 received allowances. These allowances were however inadequate; the means and credit of many failed; the small shopkeepers, instead of £9 or £10 took no more than £2 or £3 a week from the families of the workmen. The distress became in some cases urgent, yet the struggle was protracted through the rest of the year. The wives evidently thought their husbands in the right, and suffered with them the pangs of hunger. A relieving officer thus writes on September 1st, 'I visited this man's lodging; he was out, but his wife was in bed, with scarcely a rag to cover her, evidently gradually sinking from want; the room contained scarcely an article of furniture and presented a most destitute, and neglected, and dirty appearance. She said, "We are starving, sir; we have neither fire nor food." "Why," I replied, "does not your husband go to work?" "What!" she exclaimed, with considerable energy, "to become worse than a slave!"

This distress produced ultimately a sensible effect on the mortality of the men and their wives. As long as there was bread, the poor children, however, apparently had it; until weakened, cold, ill-clad, they at last died in unusual numbers as the severe weather came on towards the close of the year."

Extract from Report of Registrar-General of Births, Deaths and Marriages in England for the year 1859

DOCUMENTS IN THE CASE

On 3rd June, 1858, the delegates of the Carpenters and Joiners of London, after an aggregate meeting, sent the following letter to the Master Builders' Society:

"To the Master Builders and Employers of Carpenters and Joiners of London and its Vicinity.

GENTLEMEN, — At an aggregate meeting of the trade, held in Exeter Hall, on June 3rd, 1858, it was unanimously resolved that a memorial should be presented to you, asking you to reduce the hours of labour from ten to nine hours per day, *with the present rate of wages.*

The reason why we ask this of you is, we believe the time has come when there must be a better equalization of the hours of labour, in consequence of the great increase both of population and machinery; we are not opposed to machinery, but we are of opinion that the working classes ought to reap some benefit from its extensive introduction, and the benefit we wish is a mitigation of the hours of labour.

We also think that reducing our labour one hour per day would be a great boon to society in general, and would have a beneficial tendency to those employed in promoting their *moral and social* condition.

Gentlemen, the object of this memorial is to respectfully request you to concede to us the privilege of working nine hours per day, instead of ten (as at present). We wish this alteration to take place without any diminution in the present rate of wages; should you grant us this boon, it will produce and promote a better feeling between employer and employed, for long hours of labour are detrimental to both. Hoping you will consider this question as employers of labour belonging to a great country which is held up as a model for the admiration of the world.

We are, Gentlemen,
Yours respectfully, on behalf of the Trade Delegates,
THE COMMITTEE,
GEORGE POTTER, *Secretary."*

On 26th August the employers refused to "accede to the request made". Meanwhile the stone masons and the bricklayers joined the movement, followed by the painters and plasterers. On 19th March, 1859, after further refusals had been received, the five United Building Trades sent a further letter:

"To the Members of the Master Builders' Society.

GENTLEMEN, — We, the Conference of the Building Trades, amalgamated for the purpose of attaining the nine hours per day, deem it expedient once more to communicate with you on the issue in question. You are doubtless fully aware of the whole of our proceedings since we last addressed you, and these proceedings we are convinced cannot fail to have their due weight with yourselves. Supported as our cause is by the public press, acknowledged favourably by the Association of Architects, advocated from the pulpit, and our own energetic and persevering efforts, it cannot fail to call for your entire approval.

Your resolutions submitted to us do not express any thing definite; but to enter into debate on this question by letter would be next to impossible, and is not our intention.

This much we may be allowed to say, that we consider this movement has been agitated long enough to entitle us to claim either your sanction or rejection.

And not doubting that it has been discussed in your Association, we respectfully request an answer from your meeting, whether you will consider the nine hours as a day's work. Yes or no.

I have the honour to be, on behalf of the Conference,
Yours most respectfully,
GEORGE POTTER, *Secretary.*

19th March, 1859."

The Master Builders called a meeting on 20th April to discuss this letter, and resolved:

"That in the opinion of this meeting it is not expedient to accede to the request of the workmen contained in their letter of the 19th March, because the present arrangement of hours is the most convenient to all parties, and does not involve such an amount of time as to bring the building workmen at all within the limit of those on whose behalf the public interest has been excited, and its benevolence aroused (the hours being from six in the morning to half-past five in the afternoon, with one hour and a half interval for meals); and because much public inconvenience would result from the discontinuance of work at so early an hour as half-past four, involving, as it would do, the stoppage of all machinery, plant, and cattle, at an early hour."

To which the unions replied with an "ultimatum" (26th May):

"AN ULTIMATUM.

To the Members of the Master Builders' Association.

GENTLEMEN, — At a large meeting of the Building Trades held in Exeter Hall on the 18th instant, your resolutions were discussed, and after deep consideration we were unable to see that you have definitely answered our letter of March 19th, and we are unwilling to believe that you seriously entertain the intention of taking on yourselves the responsibility of causing the public disaster which was threatened by several of your body at your meeting on the 20th April.

We, therefore, being influenced by the most friendly feelings, once more appeal to you to consider our claim, and we respectfully request a decisive answer from your meeting on the 9th June next, *whether you will concede the nine hours as a day's work.*

I remain, Gentlemen, yours respectfully,
On behalf of the United Trades,
GEO. POTTER, *Secretary.*"

The employers again refused, whereupon the men decided to send a memorial to four building firms (drawn out of a hat). In one firm (Messrs. Trollope's) a worker presenting the memorial was dismissed (for neglect of work, said the employer). In con-sequence of this, the strike commenced, on 21st July.

"NINE HOURS' MOVEMENT.

Important Notice to the Operatives of the Building Trade.

The Master Builders having refused to concede the nine hours as a day's work, the Conference of the United Building Trades have been directed by the members of the movement to call upon a firm to cease work; having done so, they now appeal to you to aid them in supporting the men now on strike at Messrs. Trollopes'. It is earnestly hoped that no workmen will go in to supplant them till they have gained their object. It is expected that every man will do his duty.

By order of the Executive,
GEORGE POTTER, *Secretary.*"

The employers met on 27th July and heard many complaints of the tyranny and dictation of the unions, finally deciding, after long discussion:

"That the metropolitan builders are compelled to close their establishments on the 6th of August; but taking into consideration the great number of men who wholly discountenance the Confer-ence, a Committee of twenty be appointed to consider the best means of opening the doors to such men as may be willing to come to work, independent of, and not subject to, the dictation of any society interfering with the labour of the working man."

The Committee of 20 met on 1st August, and recommended that the employers should counter the trades' unions action by them-selves forming a close "Association of Metropolitan Master Builders" with the following obligatory and binding "fundamental rules":

84

"That no member of this Association shall engage, or continue in his employment, any contributor to the funds of any Trades' Union or Trades' Society which practices interference with the regulations of any establishment, the hours or terms of labour, the contracts or agreements of employers or employed, or the qualification or terms of service.

That no deputations of Trades' Unions, Committees, or other bodies, with reference to any objects referred to in article 3, be received by any member of this Association on any account whatever; it being still perfectly open to any workman, individually, to apply on such subject to his employer, who is recommended to be at all times open and accessible to any personal representation of his individual operatives.

That no member of this Association shall engage or continue in his employment any workman whomsoever until the person engaging such workman shall have stipulated with and obtained from him his distinct agreement and formal assent to the conditions embraced in the following form of engagement, which shall be read over to every such workman, and a copy whereof shall be handed to him before entering upon his work:—

'I declare that I am not now, nor will I during the continuance of my engagement with you become, a member of, or support, any society which directly or indirectly interferes with the arrangements of this or any other establishment, or the hours or terms of labour; and that I recognise the right of employers and employed individually to make any trade engagements on which they may choose to agree.'

That no member of this Association shall permit dictation, interference, or direct or indirect tampering with the management of his establishment, or the engagement, or conditions of the service of his workmen; but that, in the event of a strike or turn-out occurring in the establishment of any member of this Association from reasons or from causes which shall, in the opinion of the executive committee, entitle the employer so assailed to its countenance and support, it is hereby, and shall continue to be distinctly understood, that all the members of the Association shall sustain, according to

their power and ability, such member in upholding the objects of
the Association; it being expressly understood and declared, that
no acts shall warrant the interference of this committee except
such as it is the declared object of the foregoing provisions to
prevent.

Your Committee further recommend, that all works on which
the metropolitan Builders are engaged within the circle of the
London Postal District shall be discontinued Saturday next, the
6th August current, and that it shall be intimated to each workman that, so soon as Messrs. Trollope and Sons have resumed their
works, the other Master Builders will re-open their works on a new
agreement . . ."

*On 2nd August the Government was asked to intervene, but
refused. On 3rd August the men held a demonstration in Hyde
Park and the following resolution was carried:*

"That this meeting views with regret the position of antagonism
assumed by the employers, inasmuch as the spirit they display is
calculated to widen the breach already existing, by endeavouring to
trample out the spirit of humanity which originated, and still ani-
mates, the nine hours' movement; and as the pledge which they
would exact from us by signing the document they propose submitting, would rob us of every privilege of free men, and reduce
us to the condition of serfs, we determine to use every moral
power of resistance, and pledge ourselves to use all constitutional
measures for bringing the nine hours' movement to a successful
termination."

*On 6th August, 225 of the largest building firms in London
employing 24,000 workers, closed their shops. Attempts at mediation were unsuccessful. The lock-out was on. Large numbers of men
left London immediately to seek work in the country. Many
obtained work from the smaller builders who had not closed their*

shops. *The remainder on strike received strike pay which rarely averaged more than 3s. 6d. a week. Even this money had to be raised through meetings and subscriptions in various parts of the country.*

The strike dragged on until November, but by this time, the Nine-Hours Movement had ceased to be the main issue. This was now the demand of the masters for the "document". At the end of November, the number on strike was down to about 5,000 men. These men and their families, were literally dying of starvation, as the following table shewed;—

"The following table shows the deaths in the various branches of the building trades during three successive periods of six weeks. If the numbers in the first six weeks may be taken as the average numbers, the excess in the two following periods is considerable. Neither the additional workmen who came to town, nor the weather, will account for the whole increase.

Summary in periods of six weeks of the Deaths in five branches of the Building Trades.

Periods of Six Weeks.	Bricklayers.			Carpenters.			Masons.			Painters.			Plasterers.		
	Men.	Wives.	Children.	Men.	Wives.	Children.	Men.	Wives.	Children.	Men.	Wives.	Children.	Men.	Wives.	Children.
1859. Sept. 10 to Oct. 22.	8	5	29	24	26	105	3	2	11	26	10	51	4	1	15
Oct. 22 to Dec. 3.	19	10	30	59	22	101	9	6	16	37	67	67	6	7	11
Dec. 3 to Jan. 14, 1860.	15	12	54	47	26	135	10	6	16	42	14	50	10	6	34"

In the beginning of December a suggestion was made by Lord St. Leonards that the document be withdrawn and that, in lieu of it, there should be hung up in every shop a paper embodying the law affecting masters and men. This was a compromise which restricted the unions, while enabling them to continue in being. On 6th February, 1860, this was accepted by the Masters, and ended the lock-out and strike. The movement in favour of the nine hours was closed, or at least, postponed.

Extracts are from G. SHAW LEFEVRE's and THOMAS R. BENNET's *Account of the strike and lock-out in the Building Trades of London in 1859-60*

23. Engineers' Nine-Hours Movement, 1871

[*THE engineers in 1871 achieved their nine-hours movement with much less difficulty. Although there were strikes in Newcastle-on-Tyne and elsewhere, these were successful and they resulted in many employers granting these conditions, without dispute.*

Messrs. J. and W. Dudgeon, of Millwall, one of the largest firms in the Engineering and Iron Ship-building trade, conceded the nine-hours with this letter:]

"10, London Street, Fenchurch Street, London, E.C.
1st *December,* 1871.

GENTLEMEN, — We have every reason to be greatly pleased with the address you have presented to us to-day, coming as it does from 1,570 of our workmen, and gives not only an account of the Nine Hours' Movement, but also as the result of the good feeling that has always existed between us, there never arising any difference which we have not amicably settled.

We have summered and wintered together, and when times were not so prosperous as now you all know how in a season of utter depression, by dint of hard work, we carried our share of the Thames trade over, and may say have greatly assisted in bringing back the trade to this river.

The day of nine hours has never been a difficulty so far as we are concerned, because being workmen ourselves we know practically what 10 hours a day is when the odd quarter day is added to it; and considering that I, the head of the firm, have walked from the middle of the Commercial Road to Seward's shop for a whole bitter winter, meaning 5 o'clock in the morning and 8.30 in the evening for labour, leaving the short balance of two hours for book and drawing-board, the gain of one hour in the evening for these purposes must be invaluable.

The engineers' strike at Newcastle: arrival of foreign workmen.

In taking this address from Mr. Childs, it is a matter of great personal pleasure to me, because Mr. Childs and I have each worked the *big fire* in a large engineering establishment, and I am sure we both believe we could do so again, should the necessity for it arise.

I now, gentlemen, hand this address to my eldest son, that when his day comes, he will be able to see how his Uncle and his Father did when questions of moment arose between them and their workmen.

Signed, JOHN DUDGEON.

Mr. A. J. Dudgeon said, that should the time arrive when he succeeded his Father, he would endeavour to do as his Father had done."

*MONTHLY REPORT of Amalgamated Society
of Engineers (December, 1871)*

24. Agricultural Labourers' Lock-Outs, 1872-4

"THE condition of agricultural labourers had often been a subject of public comment during the earlier years of the present century, but it was not until 1833 that any real effort had been made to form a union. The Dorsetshire Labourers' Union of that date was squelched by the prosecution, conviction, and sentences to transportation passed upon the leaders in 1834. The terrible tale of distress and endurance among the labouring population in the various agricultural districts of England is too large a subject to be entered upon here. Some idea can be formed of the dreadful poverty, the wretched homes, and unexpressed misery to be found in vast districts, solely dependent upon agriculture, by reference to the Parliamentary inquiries in 1841-42, and 1867, and to the earlier volumes of the reports of Poor-law Boards of Commissioners, from 1834 to the date of the National Agricultural Labourers' Union in 1872.

The movement for the formation of this union began in Warwickshire, on February 12th, 1872, the first public meeting being held two days later, and a third on February 21st. Other meetings speedily followed in the locality, and early in March the labourers of Wellesbourne sent in a request to their employers for a rise in wages to 2s. 8d. per day, hours of labour to be from 6 a.m. till 5 p.m., and 3 p.m. on Saturdays, with extra for overtime, the pay for which was to be 4d. per hour. The farmers took no notice of this request, probably regarding the whole thing thus suddenly sprung upon them as a huge joke. On March 11th, however, the labourers of Wellesbourne struck, some 200 men being engaged in the strike. Some of the farmers conceded what the men demanded, others refused and proceeded to evict the cottagers from their homes. On Good Friday (March 29th, 1872) "The Warwickshire Agricultural Labourers' Union" was founded at Leamington, close

91

by. This was followed by a proposal to establish a National Union of Agricultural Labourers, the circular letter as to which was

Craft trade unionists on the march through Manchester in 1874, demonstrating against the lock-out of farm workers in Suffolk.

issued on April 27th, 1872, and sent to all parts of the kingdom. The response was so great and general that, on May 29th, a National Congress of Labourers' Delegates was convened, and was attended by representatives of twenty-six counties. At this Congress the National Union was founded. At the date of the first annual conference, held on May 28th and 29th, 1873, it was reported that twenty-six district unions had been established, with a total of 982 branches, and over 70,000 members. By 1874 the number of branches had increased to 1,000, with 10,000 members, and the *Labourers' Chronicle* had been established, which reached a circulation of 30,000 copies weekly.

The movement, so modestly begun in Warwickshire, having spread all over the country, the farmers became alarmed, and they determined to form an association to resist the demands of their labourers. But notices were served upon the farmers demanding an increase of wages in various counties, and many partial or local strikes took place. Early in 1873 several larger strikes ensued, followed by a lockout in the Eastern Counties. By means of emigration, migration, and support while on strike, the men were generally successful in obtaining the advance in wages asked for. Early in 1874 further strikes took place, followed by a lockout of 4,000 labourers, in the neighbourhood of Newmarket and adjacent districts, and also by lockouts in East Suffolk, Lincolnshire, and other places. The total cost of these great strikes and lockouts cannot be accurately given, but the union itself voted £24,432 11s. 7d. during the six months — March to August, 1874, inclusive. Besides this, the branches used their own funds, and various trades contributed liberally, the engineers giving £1,000. Public subscriptions also poured in to aid those locked out or on strike. The aggregate number on strike and locked out cannot be ascertained, but the general result was an improvement in wages all over the country."

GEORGE HOWELL, Great Strikes: Their Origin,
Cost and Results (*C.W.S. Annual 1889*)

25. A New Song, 1874

A NEW SONG ON THE LOCK-OUT OF THE
FARMERS' LABOURERS

TUNE — "*All Round the World.*"

"COME all you jolly farming men,
　　And listen to my lay,
Altho' we're not on strike again,
　　We are lock'd out I say.
Our masters they are hard on us,
　　They want to keep us down,
They want ten shillings' worth of work
　　For about half-a-crown.

Chorus.

Then all over the world in search of work we'll go,
Before we'll let the farmers keep the labourer's wages low.

For many years they've treated us
　　Much worse than any slaves;
Half-starved we pass a wretched life
　　To fill a pauper's grave:
But now we've got more sense, my boys,
　　The world we'll ramble through;
With willing hands and honest hearts
　　We'll soon find work to do.

They have lock'd the farmer's labourers out,
　　And many thousands now
In idleness must walk about
　　Instead of being at the plough.
The Agricultural Union says
　　To Harry, Bill, and Jack,
"Unite yourselves with us, my boys,
　　We'll beat them like a sack."

94

A New Song, 1874

They'll cross the broad Atlantic then
 Before they will give in;
In Canada there's work for all,
 And fortunes there to win.
Let farmers do the best they can —
 They were always greedy elves —
If they will not pay the working man,
 Why, let them work themselves.

The farmers have a Union now
 To oppose their servant-men,
But the man who whistles at the plough
 Is quite as good as them.
The men are used to hardships,
 And on purpose to get free,
They all will stand a little more —
 That the masters soon will see. .

The farmers say, "We've done our best
 For the men who till the ground;"
If they had to live as labourers do,
 They'd very soon turn round.
Altho' they've lock'd their labourers out,
 We tell them to their cheek,
Their bellies would not be so stout
 Upon twelve bob a-week."

FREDERICK CLIFFORD, *The Agricultural*
Lock-out of 1874 (1875)

26. Liverpool Seamen's Strike, 1886

"THE trouble long anticipated at Liverpool at last broke out. The men insisted on a strike, and as a matter of fact did come out on strike, quite contrary to the rules and the constitution, and we were ill-equipped with funds. I had to rush off to Liverpool and try to retrieve the situation, but it had gone too far, so with the greatest reluctance I decided to champion the cause of the men. It would have been much better if I had not done so. The fight lasted six weeks. It was a stirring and bitter fight, both the ship-owners and myself were out to win. I saw some of the principal owners at the beginning and endeavoured to have all questions settled on conciliatory lines. Many of the owners were sympathetic to this course, but the majority, I regret to say, were not so inclined. Thousands of blacklegs were procured from all parts of the country. Fishermen from Yarmouth were imported in hundreds to act as deck hands. The firemen's department was filled with men from inland towns or anywhere from whence they could be obtained.

The owners decided to have a depot ship to house the strike breakers, so they fitted up one of their old liners, "The Atlas." for the accommodation of the blacklegs. These men were landed at different places and conveyed to the depot ship. The crimps of course were very active, and I was told at the time that they were paid as much as two pounds for every man whom they recruited.

I was doomed to an exciting time. It was a difficult task to keep the men together, and I thought then as I do now, in a strike of this kind, that the men's interests should be kept centred on the objects of the strike. Tell them the truth, never deceive them. Whilst delivering my cheery speeches, I never made promises that were not likely to be fulfilled. Take the men into your confidence as much as you can, at the meetings, of course, and don't grant too many interviews to individual men, was my policy which prevented strife and jealousy. Our magnificent fight won the admiration of thousands of good Trade Unionists. Our demands were reasonable and sound arguments were used to support them. We never talked of destroying the capitalist class. The crimps were our most dangerous enemies, and I sought to win those men to our side. On one occasion I got together twelve of the most prominent crimps; they were a soulless and coldblooded lot. I endeavoured to impress upon them that the cause I was fighting for was that of the women and children. At this they laughed and sneered. They told me, however, that if I would put up a substantial sum of money they would not work against me — they did not mention the amount. I would make no such promises.

The conference with the crimps was held in the Trades Hall, situated in Brunswick Street. This was our headquarters. The meeting was supposed to be a secret one — there were myself and two or three trusted lieutenants present, in addition to the twelve sharks. But by some means or other it had got noised abroad that I had the crimps in the hall, and in less than an hour the strikers turned up in thousands outside. Fortunately, I had taken the precaution to double bar the door. The crowd began to clamour for admission and were yelling shouts of execration on the crimps. We could hear the yelling and shouts from inside. The crimps became alarmed and began to plead for mercy. I knew perfectly well that if ever that crowd got hold of the crimps not one of them would have been left to tell the tale, so I had to take immediate steps for them to escape by the windows at the rear of the premises. All the time the men were clamouring outside, and endeavouring to batter down the door, which fortunately was a strong one. When I thought that the crimps had reached a place of safety I informed those outside nearest to the door that I would come outside and address them as to how the negotiations had proceeded.

I opened the door quickly and had two or three men to close and bar it once I was outside. If ever a man or youth had to take courage in both hands I had to do so on this occasion. I have never seen before or since such an angry crowd of men. There was murder in every man's eyes, and for quite an hour it took all my efforts to appease their anger. By the time I started to address them they had several lengths of rope ready for the hanging of the crimps. Their intention was to hoist them up to a lamp-post and then riddle them with revolver shots. I knew over a dozen men in that crowd who were armed with revolvers. Occasionally I would crack a joke which would create much laughter. I knew that once they started to laugh I was on the winning side.

I then suggested that I should take a deputation of twelve inside to prove to the crowd that the crimps were not there. They were certainly a thorough search-party; every cellar and cupboard was critically examined, even to the roof. I then went out with the deputation, gave a few more encouraging words to the men, and called for three cheers for the movement and the union; then the crowd dispersed. This was a critical moment in my life and the picture of that scene is vividly brought back to my mind as I sit writing these lines . . .

A large number of anonymous letters appeared in the Press, which were supposed to have come from seamen's wives, condemning the strike, and myself in particular. I thought this might have an effect on public opinion, which I was anxious to have on my side. So I immediately convened a meeting of women, the wives and relatives of seamen, to be held in a large hall in Lord Nelson Street. There were nearly two thousand. No males were admitted except myself. The women looked a sturdy crowd. I asked them to appoint their own Chairwoman. This was speedily done, and the one selected was about forty or forty-five, who could talk very well.

I explained the causes that had led to the strike, and left it to the women to decide what should be our future policy. Many of the women addressed the meeting in short speeches, and a resolution was moved and seconded that they stand by their men-folk. This was carried amidst great enthusiasm. This move on my part killed the anonymous letter writing, and we heard no more of it.

The strike was now in its fourth week; the men were still fresh and determined. I saw, however, that we were doomed to failure because the supply of strike breakers was inexhaustible. Many exciting adventures befell me in capturing these men. I would be informed by telegram that two or three hundred men were leaving Yarmouth by certain trains for Liverpool.

I would take a train down the line where they would have to change at some junction, and I was often successful in getting in touch with the men on the journey to Liverpool. I would plead with them the cause of Liverpool seamen. By this means I captured as many as fifty in a batch. However, those in charge on the employers' side soon learnt of this, and special trains were engaged, with all the doors of the carriages locked. Special instructions were given to the stationmasters that should the trains stop at any station no one was to be allowed to board them.

The men I managed to get from the other side were very costly, for we had to pay their lodging expenses in Liverpool, and then the train fares back to their homes. This made big inroads on our already depleted treasury. At the end of the fifth week a proclamation was issued by the employers to the effect that on and after a certain date the whole of the men on strike would be barred for ever from employment in the Company's service. I knew perfectly well that this threat could never be carried out, as the officers of the ships were reporting from time to time what a terrible experience they were having with the blacklegs, especially the engineers, as many of the new firemen had never been to sea previously. There were no oil-burning ships, it was all coal-burning, and it required men with skill as well as strength to get those Atlantic greyhounds through the water.

In addition to the bar against the men returning to the ships, there was another proviso to the effect that the men would have to renounce their union and sign an agreement to that effect. This movement on the part of the owners required that I should act quickly, and I think my tactics achieved their purpose in every part of Liverpool. I convened private meetings of the men and went into the question very thoroughly. I discovered how wise I had been in never promising the men too much, but that at every stage of the fight I had told them "Whenever you chaps think you have reached the limit of your resources, let me know and I will close down at once." I was also very particular to take ballots from

99

time to time to ascertain the true feeling of the men. In this I was most particular, so that when a man recorded his vote his neighbours had no possible chance of knowing which way he cast it. This was a useful guide to me; not one per cent. of the men wavered. I have heard some people say that Liverpool men could never put up a fight, but I have always laughed at this idea. The best fighters that I met with in any part of the world were the Liverpool men; but one had to be exceedingly careful in handling them. They must not be told lies — their confidence must be retained, and they will follow their leaders to death.

When the employers' ultimatum was issued I resolved that the men should return to work triumphantly in a solid body, so I called special meetings in all districts, and told the men, as their leader, that in my opinion they could not succeed on that occasion, and strongly advised them to call the strike "off." I explained carefully what I wanted them to do. I was going to take a ballot that evening and wanted every man to vote solidly in favour of the strike. Next morning they were to present themselves at their ships in a body. I had taken the trouble to keep the Press well informed that the strike ballot was unanimously in favour of continuing the strike, which was perfectly true, not one man dissented, and of course, the papers announced the result of the ballot and the determination of the men to carry on. So the following morning, when the men presented themselves at their ships in large numbers, the general opinion on the other side was that the men had broken their allegiance to the union. Some thousands were taken on that morning, and the strike-breakers were cleared out. My men were jubilant over this move. The men rallied to the union, and not long after their wages were increased considerably, but I could not get the owners to adopt the Conciliation Board. I have no doubt their feeling was that I was a very bad member of society, and they were not prepared to trust me . . ."

J. HAVELOCK WILSON (President, National Sailors' and Firemen's Union) *My Stormy Voyage through Life* (1925)

27. The Match Girls' Strike, 1888

"AT A meeting of the Fabian Society, Miss Clementina Black gave a capital lecture on Female Labour, and urged the formation of a Consumers League, pledged only to buy from shops certificated "clean" from unfair wage. H. H. Champion, in the discussion that followed, drew attention to the wages paid by Bryant & May (Ltd.), while paying an enormous dividend to their shareholders, so that the value of the original £5 shares was quoted at £18 7s. 6d. Herbert Burrows and I interviewed some of the girls, got lists of wages, of fines, etc. A typical case is that of a girl of 16, a piece-worker; she earns 4/- a week, and lives with a sister, employed by the same firm, who "earns good money, as much as 8/- or 9/- a week". Out of the earnings 2/- a week is paid for the rent of one room. The child lives only on bread and butter and tea, alike for breakfast and dinner, but related with dancing eyes that once a month she went to a meal where "you get coffee and bread and butter, and jam and marmalade, and lots of it". We published the facts under the title of "White Slavery in London", and called for a boycott of Bryant and May's Matches. "It is time someone came and helped us," said two pale-faced girls to me; and I asked: "Who will help?" Plenty of people wish well to any good cause; but very few care to exert themselves to help it, and still fewer will risk anything in its support. "Someone ought to do it, but why should I", is the ever re-echoed phrase of weak-kneed amiability. "Someone ought to do it, so why NOT I?", is the cry of some earnest servant of man, eagerly forward springing to face perilous duty. Between those two sentences lie whole centuries of moral evolution.

I was promptly threatened with an action for libel, but nothing came of it; It was easier to strike at the girls, and a few days later, Fleet Street was enlivened by the irruption of a crowd of Match Girls, demanding Annie Besant. I couldn't speechify the Match Girls to Match Girls in Fleet Street, so asked that a deputation

Members of the Matchmakers' Union.

should come and explain what they wanted. Up came three women
and told their story: They had been asked to sign a paper, certify-
ing that they were well treated, and contented, and that my state-
ments were untrue; they refused. "You had spoke up for us," explained one, "and we weren't going back on you." A girl, pitched
on as their leader, was threatened with dismissal; she stood firm;
next day she was discharged for some trifle, and they all threw
down their work, some 1,400 of them, and then a crowd of them

102

started off to me to ask what to do next. If we ever worked in our lives, Herbert Burrows and I worked for the next fortnight. And a pretty hubbub we created; we asked for money, and it came pouring in; we registered the girls to receive strike pay, wrote articles, roused the Club, held public meetings, got Mr. Bradlaugh to ask questions in Parliament, stirred up constituencies in which shareholders were members, till the whole country rang with the struggle. Mr. Frederick Charrington lent us a hall for registration; Mr. Sidney Webb and others moved the National Liberal Club to action; we led a procession of the girls to the House of Commons, and interviewed with a deputation of them, Members of Parliament, who cross-questioned them. The girls behaved splendidly, stuck together, kept brace and bright all through. Mr. Hobart of the Social Democratic Federation, Messrs. Shaw, Bland and Oliver, and Headlam of the Fabian Society, Miss Clementina Black and many another, helped in the heavy work. The London Trades Council finally consented to act as arbitrators, and a satisfactory settlement was arrived at; the girls went into work, fines and deductions were abolished, better wages paid; the Matchmakers Union was established, still the strongest Woman's Trades Union in England, and for years I acted as Secretary, till, under press of other duties, I resigned, and my work was given by the girls to Mrs. Thornton Smith; Herbert Burrows became, and still is, the Treasurer. For a time there was friction between the Company and the Union, but it gradually disappeared under the influence of commonsense on both sides, and we have found the manager ready to consider any just grievance and to endeavour to remove it, while the Company have been liberal supporters of the Working Women's Club at Bow, founded by H. P. Blavatsky.

The worst suffering of all was among Boxmakers, thrown out of work by the Strike, and they were hard to reach. 2¼d. per gross of boxes, and buy your own string and paste, is not wealth, but when the work went, more rapid starvation came. Oh, those trudges through the lanes and alleys round Bethnal Green Junction late at night, when our day's work was over; children lying about on shavings, rags, anything; famine looking out of baby faces, out of women's eyes, out of the tremulous hands of men. Heart grew sick and eyes dim, and ever louder sounded the question, "Where is the cure for sorrow, what the way of rescue for the world?"

In August, I asked for a "Match Girls' Drawing Room." "It will want a piano, tables for papers, for games, for light literature; so that it may offer a bright, homelike refuge to these girls, who now have no real homes, no playground save the streets. It is not proposed to build an "institution" with stern and rigid discipline and enforcement of prim behaviour, but to open a home filled with the genial atmosphere of cordial comradeship, and self-respecting freedom — the atmosphere so familiar to all who have grown up in the blessed shelter of a happy home, so strange, alas! to too many of our East London girls". In the same month of August, two years later, H. P. Blavatsky opened such a home."

ANNIE BESANT, *Autobiography* (1893 ed.)

28. The Great Dock Strike, 1889

[*TEN THOUSAND London dockers came out for a wage of sixpence an hour, special payment for overtime and the abolition of piece-work. The strike lasted a month. Nearly £50,000 was raised by public subscription. Finally practically the whole of the dockers' demands were conceded. The "Docker's tanner" became an accomplished fact.*]

THE CARDINAL AND THE STRIKERS

". . . In truth a strike is like a battle. No one who was in it can give an account of it. Each man knows only the events on the spot where he stood. Time and distance are necessary for a complete outline and description. And these are generally better understood by those who have watched the fray without sharing it.

About the Strike I can say nothing but what everybody knows already; certain facts, however, have forced themselves upon me in the following order:—

First, the immense suffering which falls in a moment on women and children; and the ruin of careful thrift, which is drawn out from savings banks and prudential societies. Moreover, there is ruin among the lesser tradesmen; and a bar to the importation of food. A strike makes bankrupts of tens of thousands of the most deserving of our people.

Secondly, the unknown dangers which in a moment might, by the act of a fool, or a madman, or a malefactor, be let loose upon us. Once begun, no one could foresee the end.

Thirdly, the spread of a restless sympathy in the labour market all over the land, and especially in the chief centres of industry.

Fourthly, the almost certain injury permanently inflicted upon the Port of London. It is a proverb that capital, like fish, is shy. Once frightened away it will not return. Commerce is capital in

A float in one of the processions during the Great Dock Strike. The REMEDY of the Doctor (the Employers) for the state of London Docks was to cut wages, whitewash their actions and send the docker to the pawnshop.

activity. London now only holds its own with difficulty in competition with Southampton, Cardiff, Liverpool, Glasgow, and Hull, and even with Antwerp and the French ports.

What we may hope will come from this strike is a registration of labourers and an organisation of labour. This will clear the dock gates and the East of London of thousands who year by year flow in from the country without knowledge or skill. They become a floating population of disappointed men; indolent because unemployed, living from hand to mouth, and dangerous because they have nothing to lose: starving in the midst of wealth and prosperity from which they are excluded.

Nevertheless, without any blind self-praise, I believe we may say that since the Cotton Famine of the North there has been no nobler example of self-command than we have seen in the last month.

And I am bound to bear witness not only to the self-command of the men, but also to the measured language and calm courtesy of the employers. They have maintained an attitude of resistance to what they judged to be excessive, or, at least, inconsistent with the grave interest of those for whom they were trustees. Now, happily reconciled, the conduct on both sides gives the surest pledge of peace; and of mutual and permanent welfare.

Slight disorders here and there were inevitable and foreseen. The seeds of them were sown before the Strike. They sprang up after it, not from it, and by wise policy will soon cease to exist."

CARDINAL MANNING (*New Review,*
October 1889)

JOHN BURNS' ACCOUNT

". . . It is now some six years since John Williams, myself, and others, commenced our crusade amongst the dockers. A crusade of the dawn, I may call it; for we did our haranguing amongst the men in the hours of the morning before their work and ours had commenced. I myself, with my wife, have frequently left home at three and four o'clock in the morning, winter and summer; tramped to the docks, made speeches at three different gates, and returned to begin my day's work in the West End at seven or eight o'clock. I have done this for weeks and months together; I was doing it at intervals through the years 1884, 1885, and 1886.

It was in this way that I came to know the men familiarly, and they to know me. Some of these men had been at school with me, some of them had worked under me in the docks — for I, too, have done my turn there, at my trade of engineer. We who were thus openly agitating and spreading discontent in this neglected corner of the world of labour, learned thoroughly the whole condition, economic and social, of the various classes of dock labourers; saw how wretched it was, and deliberately set ourselves to make the men revolt against their lot. That, in the end, we succeeded in doing so, says quite as much, I fancy, for the quality of the men

107

themselves as for the resolute and persistent efforts of those who, when they had got the crusade into life, kept it steadily, and continuously, and resistlessly going. If the stuff we had to work upon had been such stuff as the dock labourer was once thought to be compounded of, we might have stood on tubs at every dock gate in turn, and talked the tongues out of our mouths – there would have been no strike. It is not to me, nor to any other apostle of discontent, that the strike was mainly owing. It owed more than all else to the fact – now patent to the world – that the dock labourer is a man radically different from the creature of whilom popular imagination. "The forlorn hope of the army of labour" he always was; but neither degraded nor a loafer, No; they were not loafers with whom we had to deal. There is no "strike" in the loafer. It is a fool's mission to preach revolt to *him*. It is the task of the priests of Baal trying to call down fire from Heaven; of Don Quixote seeking to make a knight-errant of Sancho Panza. The coals we blew upon were working-men; oppressed, beaten down; but working-men still, who had it in them to struggle, and to fight, for their daily bread. Is it the loafer by trade, do you think, who is willing to shiver for hours under the dock gates, in the black gelidity of a December morning, for the chance of a shillingsworth of work, and work that needs as much muscle as will? I have seen dock hands fighting for the gates, like people tussling in the passages of a burning theatre: the fierce physical energy (moral inspiration apart) which the chronic loafer, even if he would, is powerless to exert.

Again, a strike of loafers (were the thing conceivable) would have been no such disciplined and mannerly affair as this has been. A hundred thousand loafers would not have roamed the streets on strike and given no trouble to the police, and stolen less even than Garibaldi's Red-shirts in their march through Calabria upon Naples. When trouble is abroad it is, one may say, the duty of the loafer to make it worse; for that way his profits lie. The honest worker in such a crisis knows how to efface himself for the good of his class. We knew well enough it was with the honest workers that our account lay in this movement. And, perceiving that the hopelessly casual nature of their employment made their standard rate of pay an utterly inadequate one, we perceived also that in organised action lay their only hope of bettering their wages. This was the point we thrust home on all occasions.

At this particular period, and still earlier, I was actively concerned in the spreading movement of the unemployed throughout the whole of the East End of London. Working thirteen hours a day for my own bread and cheese, at Brotherhood's, in Westminster, I made time to do something as a Socialist propagandist, and formed, or helped to form, several new trade unions in various parts of London. The last and most important of these was the Gas Stokers' Trade Union, which numbers now 11,000 men, who, within the last four months, have succeeded in obtaining a slightly better wage for an eight hours' day than they had been receiving for a day of twelve and thirteen hours. This episode of the new trade unions is a necessary note of my narrative, for it leads directly up to the Dockers' Strike.

Many of the meetings of the Gas Stokers' Union were held in the East End, in the neighbourhood of the docks. The dockers came in numbers, and Mr. Mann, Mr. Champion, and myself addressed thousands of them. They caught the spirit that we were trying to inform them with; and when the gas workers had won their victory, the dockers in their turn became restless. It was that victory, in a word, that induced the strike of the dockers.

An old and settled dock hand, named Harris, appealed to me to form a permanent dock hands' trade union. I consented, and held a meeting of two thousand men, at which many members were enrolled. These were men who had refused to join the old dockers' union, which, from one cause and another, had ceased to be worth its name. But the information of the new union forced the old one into an activity which it had not theretofore displayed; and of this unwonted activity the immediate outcome was the strike in the South Dock on August 13th. Some 300 men came out, refusing to work any longer for 5d. an hour.

On Wednesday, August 14th, Mr. Mann went down, on a telegraphic summons, to address the men. On the day following, I presented myself at the West India Docks, to render what help I could. Discontent was simmering; I spoke to the men, and found them eager and receptive. The end we had been striving after was coming into view. Some of the stevedores were not clear as to whether they should come out or not; and said as much. I opposed them vehemently, and the meeting — 4,000 strong, at least — supported me. The stevedores gave way: they would come out, they said; and they came. From that moment the whole body of the stevedores stood to us through thick and thin, and were our sturdiest helpers. This meeting of 4,000 dockers I look back to as the real commencement of the Strike. The idea of it had now gone abroad; it was the general talk; it had "caught on"; it had taken hold of the dockers' mind. This was something; for the docker had thought himself isolated and solitary in the East. The notion of combination — which, in all days to come, is to be the watchword of labour — had been hard to drive into him. It is a notion difficult always to instil into men who, while accustomed to take the dole of capital, have been fearful of asking themselves whether it were their only due. But we had warmed them up now, and they knew that it was a question of combination or nothing. This conviction had to be widely spread; it must be made common to all of them; and on Thursday, Friday, and Saturday, August 15th, 16th, and 17th, I spoke thirty-six times — outside of wharves, docks, and warehouses, Mr. Mann, Mr. Tillett, and Mr. Champion did as much. We put the match to every corner of the building — sitting on walls, or standing astride of palings.

The *Saturday Review,* by the way, does us a small injustice in its insinuation of the tub. I should have welcomed a tub often, had there been a tub convenient; but not a tub was used throughout the Strike. They did not even roll us out a barrel from the docks. The Strike, from first to last, was full of surprises to me; and it is — as far as I remember — the first revolt of its kind that has dispensed with the legendary platform of the demagogue. When the Strike was two days advanced, the stevedores took upon them to marshal and organise the men; no light undertaking, for recruits poured in at every hour, by fifties and by hundreds. In a little while the stevedores and the dockers were no more than units amongst the mass of strikers. The coal porters came out, the lightermen pressed after them; one trade called out another; we had at one time 100,000 men on strike.

The strain that was thus put upon the leaders is scarcely to be conceived. The economic questions of the Strike seemed for a moment to sink into nothingness in comparison with the question of the commissariat. We had to find food for 250,000 stomachs every day of the week. We formed committees; and the committees, and the relief committees, had to sit through the day and the night. There was not an hour out of the twenty-four at which two or more representatives of the Central Strike Committee were not to be found at their posts. When I went into the streets, hunger made its mute appeal to me at every turn. It is this that is so sad in every strike. There are moments when one asks if it be really worth while — if it be not better that the labourer should be let alone, to take his accustomed dole, and eke it out from day to day, as he has been used to do. This is a foolish sentiment, which half an hour of cool reflection disposes of. Every faith must have its martyrs, every victory its slain. The capacity of self-sacrifice is the Philosopher's Stone that every agitator seeks for. He is powerless until he finds it; finding it, he has no more to ask. This power of self-sacrifice has been the great note of the Dockers' Strike. It was a lever the like and strength of which I had not had in my hand before, in any strike that I had helped in. If I could have put the hunger question from me, I should have been easy, knowing that I had to deal with men who were equal to the utmost of endurance.

But the very willingness of the men and their women to make nothing of the nip of hunger (perhaps the final test of endurance) pricked us to use our best to keep them in daily bread. We sent out appeals, none too confidently at the first, but with increasing confidence as the days went on. I myself was astonished at the inpouring of public money. No appeal of strikers ever drew such continuous solid help before. Literally, we asked and we received.

It seemed that we had only to say in the baldest terms that we were the dockers' treasurers, and the moneys that we asked for were forthcoming. Had ours been a Mansion House appeal on behalf of the sufferers by some sudden great disaster at home or abroad, it could not have been responded to with more extravagant generosity. Australia's subscription of £25,000 is known. In England, union after union pelted us with cheques; and every cheque was accompanied by an assurance that contributions would not be lacking, whether the Strike lasted for weeks or for months. The Compositors sent us £500; the Engineers £700.

The Strike being well forward, we had to face the difficult task of the organisation of relief. We had a population to find food for every day. On what principle should our commissariat be established? We took the East End shopkeepers into our confidence, and issued tickets presentable to them. This ticket system put an immediate check upon many possible abuses of our general plan of relief. Refusing to give money, we ensured ourselves against drunkenness and all the troubles arising out of it; troubles which have been the ruin of more strikes than one. This has been the soberest strike that I remember. From first to last, no man has asked me for money for beer. The abuse of relief was scarcely possible under the system that we instituted – a system whose maintenance we insisted upon from the first day to the last. That we were able to carry out our orders on this particular point is something to our own credit, and a great deal more to the credit of the men we had in hand.

What surprised me, too, was the readiness with which other trades, whose grievances had not before been bruited, came forward to back the dockers. That 'there were, here and there, in all parts of London, labourers in different callings who were dissatisfied with their condition, I knew well enough. But I had not looked to these men to furnish us with the sinews of war; still less had I fancied that they would turn out with the dockers in the streets. But they did so; and the recruits from the outer world of labour – who had no immediate interest in the strike of the dock workers – were amongst our most valuable assistants. They gave a moral strength to the movement. Hundreds of the men who marched the streets with the dockers had nothing to expect from their adhesion to the movement; but all of those men represented a department in the service of labour, and their trades have gained not a little by the success of the dockers.

We took account of all the trades that had lent us help, and the successful issue of the lesser strikes that have followed the strike of the dockers is traceable in no small measure to the all but overwhelming influence of the first great movement.

Carmen employed by the Post Office have secured rises of from one shilling to four shillings per week; and almost every carman employed throughout the whole East End of London has gained somewhat. The workers in the chemical manufactories along the banks of the Thames, the engineering labourers, and, in all, some 200 trades in London, have gained a full 10 per cent. on their old wages, and shorter hours, by the Dockers' Strike. Shunters, porters, and a host of labourers, not directly connected with the docks, have secured their benefits.

Lately as the Strike has ended, new movements have grown out of it. Let me pause a moment to note how warm and widespread was the support that we received all through the East of London. A sort of antagonism has been imagined as dividing the East End shopkeeper from the East End labourer. But in this Strike the shopkeepers have been amongst our most generous supporters. When I talk of East End shopkeepers I am thinking chiefly of the pawnbrokers. Five pawnbrokers out of six in the East End issued notices to the effect that they would charge no interest on articles pledged with them during the Strike; and lodging-house keepers remitted their rent during the same period. The whole East End rose and stood up alongside of us.

From the moment that we were certain of our organisation we had not a doubt as to the issue of the event. We had but to feed the men to the end, and the rest was assured. We fed them, and the day was ours.

I must turn now for a moment to generalities. I am asked, What is the net result of the Strike? I can answer in a word. The strikers have gained 1d. per hour on ordinary time; 3d. per hour from 6 to 8 p.m.; 2d. per hour after 8; whilst the four hours' call for 2s. pay gives a permanency that has only now been secured. Contract has been abolished. By the abolition of contract the men cease to be sweated by the gangers, as they have been hitherto. The contract system had been a material injury to the men throughout. We have given that system its quietus, and by so doing have removed a hundred causes of discontent and anxiety from the dock labourers. What other result has the Strike accomplished? It has destroyed now and for all time the system of sweating under which the docker found himself compelled to labour at starvation wages for the profit of his employer. It has abolished, or done much to abolish, jealousy and bad feeling of every sort amongst the dockers as a body. The brutal relations (I can give them no other name) that have existed between foremen and men have disappeared, or are bound to disappear in the immediate future. And, touching the relations of the men with their employers, those also will of necessity be bettered, inasmuch as the employers, dreading another strike, will have a substantial motive for keeping on the best possible terms with their men. Hitherto the relations of employers and men all through the docks have been degrading to the men. It will not be so in the future.

Must I say a word as to the relations of the leaders of the Strike with the representatives of the dock companies? Now that the victory has been gained I am as anxious to say as little as possible. But, as an old agitator, I am bound to express my own personal feeling that in this strike I have had to deal with men who, from first to last, seemed to me to have a very imperfect appreciation of their own best interests, and very little regard for the feelings of others. More than this, I might say that the representatives of the dock companies never seemed to me to know their own business. It is not the first time that I have had to deal with employers as antagonists to the claims of labour; but in my dozen years of agitation I do not remember to have had relations with men more completely imbued with the spirit of pure "cussedness."

What then is our immediate position on the issue of the Strike?

The gain in wages I have already touched on. That is not the most important result to be considered. We have to note, above all, that labour throughout the whole East End of London has, by the outcome of this Strike, been placed upon a higher and more substantial footing with regard to capital than it has ever stood upon before. Still more important, perhaps, is the fact that labour of the humbler kind has shown its capacity to organise itself; its solidarity; its ability; its readiness to endure much for little gain. Then, the labourer in the East has acquired hope. He has learned that combination can lead him to anything and everything. He has tasted success as the immediate fruit of combination, and he knows that the harvest he has just reaped is not the utmost he can look to gain. He has learned the value of self-sacrifice in a large movement for the benefit of his class. Conquering himself, he has learned that he can conquer the world of capital, whose generals have been the most ruthless of his oppressors.

I have never ceased to wonder all through the Strike at the moderation and the honesty of the strikers. I have been in the thick of starving men, with hundreds of pounds about me (they knowing it), and not a penny have I lost. I have sent men whom I did not know, for change of a gold piece, and have never been cheated of a penny. Not a man through all the weeks of that desperate Strike ever asked me for drink money. I have learned by things like these that the educational value of the Strike has not been inconsiderable. I saw no drunken striker in any procession; I heard no one cadging for charity. One instance of the high spirit of these dockers occurs to me. A friend came from the West to search for me. He fell in with a striker, who walked with him two miles to the committee-rooms, and refused to accept a shilling for his services as guide. We had to deal throughout with men who were capable of this sort of self-repression, and it was because we had such stuff at our backs that we were able in the end to bring our opponents to terms.

A hundred things escape me that I might set down as showing the sympathy of the community; but I remember how generously all classes have acted towards us — the East End shopkeepers, and the pawnbrokers who refused to charge interest on goods pledged with them during the Strike; the landlords and lodging-house keepers who refused rent during the same period. I remember the subscriptions of sailors, soldiers, policemen, fishermen, and the blind men of Southwark. I remember the letters (with cheques enclosed) of noblemen, club-men, and clergymen. I remember the half-sovereign which an officer of the Guards gave me in the Park, with a half-uttered suggestion that if he were called upon to act against the strikers he would give them "blank cartridge." I remember that out of the thousands of letters I received from every part of the kingdom, there were two abusive ones, and two only.

As a Trade Unionist, my own notion as to the practical outcome of the Strike is that all sections of labour must organise themselves into trades unions; that all trades must federate themselves, and that in the future, prompt and concerted action must take the place of the spasmodic and isolated action of the past.

As a Socialist, I rejoice that organised labour has shown how fully it can meet the forces of Capitalism, and how small a chance the oppressor of labour has against the resolute combination of men who, having found their ideal, are determined to realise it."

JOHN BURNS (*New Review,* October 1889)

29. The Gas-Workers' Strike, 1889

"A STRIKE has just commenced that seems likely to be of as much importance as the Dockers' Strike of 1889. It is the strike of the gas workers. As there is much misunderstanding and misrepresentation about the nature of the Gas Workers and General Labourers' Union the founders and officials of it take this opportunity of giving the public the facts of the origin and history of the Union.

As far back as 1872 the gas workers made attempts to better their position. There was a very general feeling even then that they were everywhere doing excessive work, and in 1872 the men struck. But there was no real organisation, and not much good was done except that the men learnt from their failure the necessity of organisation. In 1872 all that happened pretty much, was that the men changed stations, going from one set of works to another. One consequence of the 1872 movement was the passing of the what we call the Conspiracy Act, one provision of which, is that gas workers throwing up their work are liable to imprisonment.

The actual date of the formation of the Union was March 12th, 1889, so that it is not yet a year old. The direct cause of its forming was the Beckton strike. Beckton is in Essex, the next station on the Woolwich line after the Royal Albert Docks, and just before you come to Silvertown. The Beckton men demanded the eight hours working day, and then many other men in other gas works made the same demand. We feel bound to say that while the first fight was with the Beckton Company, and while this company was at first very much opposed to us, since they conceded our demands they have loyally adhered to all their promises and have always met us in the fairest spirit, and that the treatment of the men at Beckton compares very favourably with that meted out by some of the other companies.

From March the 12th when the first "Indignation meeting" was held, to July we were organising the Union. The founders were William Thorne and Mark Hutchins. The first of these is

117

General Secretary, the second, President of the Union. We must especially mention as energetic workers the names of Hobart, Angle, Tillett, Canty, Mann, Burns, and Gilbey.

In July the South Metropolitan Company granted the 8 hours demand, and within a fortnight all the other side of the water also granted it. And one of the most important things is that this reduction of working time was not accompanied with any reduction of wages generally. In many cases the decrease of time was accomplished with an increase of wage, and of course, it is clear that where only the same wage is paid for eight hours as was formerly paid for twelve there is a rise of wage. From that time things were pretty quiet up to September 20th. We went on with the organising work, but on September 20th, certain men were discharged from the South Metropolitan Works. As the men in the works thought the discharge unfair, they all gave in their notices. The upshot of the struggle was that the Company had to give way, that the notices were withdrawn, the men reinstated and actually paid their wages for the time they were out on strike. Then an agreement was drawn up, between the masters and the men, granting to the latter what they considered their reasonable demands. Besides this victory at the South Metropolitan and others gained in London, we may mention among others those won at Leeds, Bristol, Sunderland, Nottingham, Sheffield, Bury, Jarrow-on-Tyne, North Shields, Wakefield, Dewsbury, Barnsley, and many more.

Then came the "Great Strike." And it is no exaggeration to say that it would never have taken place but for the Gas Workers' Union. That such "unskilled workers" as the gas stokers should in a few months be able to enroll some 20,000 to 30,000 members, that they should gain an eight hours working day, increase of wage, and other concessions put heart into the dockers. Many of the "dockies" come into the gas works during the winter months. What was possible for the gas stokers was surely not impossible for them — and the dock strike was begun. The history of that strike is so recent, and so well known that we need say nothing about it here.

This brings us to the next "big" question — the abolition of Sunday labour. The formulation that this should be abolished occurred at a meeting of delegates from the various branches of the Union in October last. A resolution to put down Sunday work was then passed, and it was to come into force on November 10th. Of course the only way to get rid of Sunday labour is to have more men working, or by men working longer on Saturdays, so that there may be an extra supply of gas ready. On November 3rd our representatives had an interview with the engineers of the Companies — Mr. Jones, Mr. Livesey, etc., at Cannon Street. They there agreed to give double time, 12 hours. On November 10th we met them again, and they granted double time, 16 hours. Mr. Livesey was not at this November 10th meeting, and we understand him to have said that he would have to grant what the other engineers had agreed to, but would take it away as soon as possible. Anyhow, on the Friday after, *i.e.,* November 15th, he launched his bonus scheme, or, as we call it, bogus. We conscientiously believe that this scheme is an attempt, as Mr. Livesey is himself reported to have said, to break up our Union. If it is genuinely meant for the benefit of the workers, why cannot the "bonus" scheme be hung up for our consideration, or the equivalent be paid weekly in wages? And why are men to bind themselves as slaves to Mr. Livesey for twelve months? Above all, why if the scheme is proposed solely to benefit the workers should it be forced upon them against their will?

Our Union, as its full name implies, is not one of gas workers only, but of "unskilled" labourers generally. We should like also to point out that the term "unskilled" is misleading. It takes long years of hard work to do most of this "unskilled" work well. But accepting this term of "unskilled," our union is one for "general" or "unskilled workers." And we think that the organisation of these workers is of the utmost importance to the labour movement generally. It is really more important than the organisation of the skilled workers, since it is in the ranks of the unskilled that the employer recruits his army in times of labour troubles. Until now the unskilled have been looked down upon — and are looked down upon — by many of the skilled artisans. But our Union is going to show that the unskilled workers must henceforth be reckoned with; it will show both employers and the aristocrats of labour that they are the real power. For this reason the Gas workers' is also a General Labourers' Union. Moreover it is wholly and solely a fighting body. Our Union is not to degenerate into a mere burial and benefit society. The benefits we confer are in the shape of shorter hours of labour, better wages, healthier conditions of work. We pay out only strike money (the strikers having, of course, to consult the Union, and receive permission before striking) or support men and women dismissed from their situations for actively aiding the Union. The money paid in weekly fees and entrance fees goes for Union purposes only. We have no desire to hoard, and ours is the only Union that is a union pure and simple, and no benefit society at the same time. The consequence is that men and women join us for no merely selfish ends. We certainly want and will help ourselves — but only that we in turn may help others.

Our Union is also one of the very few in which men and women are on equal terms. We want unions of *workers* not of working *men* or working *women*. About three months ago Mrs. Aveling started a Women's Union at Silvertown, and asked if they would be admitted as a branch of the G. W. & G. L. U. At a meeting where 3,000 men were present her question was answered unanimously and enthusiastically in the affirmative. Since this, Female Branches — and very flourishing ones — have been organised in London and Bristol. As women's wages are for the most part far worse than those of men, it has been decided that they shall pay half the sums paid by men as entrance and weekly fees, and receive half the sum paid men for strike money, etc. Otherwise men and women are on an equal footing. Their branches are represented at our delegate meetings, they vote as the men, and on the committee just appointed to revise our rules there are two women. We think this true Women's Rights so far as the working class is concerned.

The work we have done in less than twelve months is this. We have enrolled over 50,000 workers, hitherto absolutely unorganised. We have gained for 80,000 men an eight instead of a twelve hour working day, which means — to take only the East End of London — the employment of 5,000 more men this winter, *i.e.*, some 20,000 less starving men, women and children. We are everywhere showing men and women the necessity of union. We are forcing the skilled mechanic to recognise the rights and claims of the "unskilled" worker and are daily, hourly enrolling more members.

With regard to the strike at the South Metropolitan Works, the responsibility rests entirely with the Company. Our men had no desire to strike. The strike was forced upon them. We are fighting for the principles of Trade Unionism, and for the right of combination, and we have the sympathy of all organized workers; and Mr. Livesey, and especially Mr. Morton, will find that a Union like ours will not allow itself to be smashed.

We put these facts before the public in the hope that we shall thus lessen the chance of the public being misled by the — we are obliged to call it so — wilful misrepresentation of some of the representatives of the gas companies. All we want is a fair hearing and fair play."

MARK HUTCHINS, *President.*
WILLIAM THORNE, *General Secretary.*

TIME. *A Monthly Magazine* (January 1890)

30. The Durham Lock-Out, 1891

[IN THE years between 1888 and 1893 the Durham coalfield was more idle than working because of the militancy of the miners over too many cut-backs in pay. During this period the membership of the Miners' Association grew from 36,000 to 200,000. The Great Durham Lock-out began in March 1892. A fall in coal prices led the owners to propose a 10% wage reduction. The men refused and were locked out. After six weeks, by which time the miners' families were starving, the colliers agreed to accept the wage cut, whereupon the owners now demanded 13½%. It would appear Tommy Armstrong (1848-1919) wrote "The Durham Lock-out" at this point. The men refused to take this further cut and the strike dragged on until a cut of 10% was finally agreed.

"THE DURHAM LOCKOUT"

"In our Durham County I am sorry for to say,
That hunger and starvation is increasing every day,
For the want of food and coals, we know not what to do,
But with your kind assistance we will stand the struggle
    through.

I need not state the reason why we have been brought so
    low,
The masters have behaved unkind, which everyone will
    know;
Because we won't lie down and let them treat us as they
    like,
To punish us, they've stopped the pits and caused the
    present strike.

122

Durham miners outside the 'B' pit at Hebburn.

May every Durham colliery owner that is in the fault,
Receive nine lashes with the rod, and then be rubbed with
    salt.
May his back be thick with boils so that he may never sit,
And never burst until the wheels go round at every pit.

The pulley wheels have ceased to move which went so
    swift around,
The horses and the ponies too all brought from
    underground,

Our work is taken from us now, they care not if we die,
For they can eat the best of food, and drink the best
     when dry.

The miner and his wife too, each morning have to roam,
To seek for bread to feed the hungry little ones at home.
The flour barrel is empty now, their true and faithful friend,
Which makes the thousands wish today the strike was at an
     end.

We have done our very best as honest working men.
To let the pits commence again, we've offered to them ten.
The offer they will no accept, they firmly do demand
Thirteen and a half per cent, or let the colliers stand.

Let them stand or let them lie or do with them as they
     choose,
To give them thirteen and a half we ever shall refuse.
They're always willing to receive, but not inclined to give.
Very soon they won't allow a working man to live.

With tyranny and capital they never seem content,
Unless they are endeavouring to take from us per cent.
If it was due, what they request, we willingly would
     grant;
We know it's not, therefore we cannot give them what
     they want.

The miners of Northumberland we shall for ever praise,
For being so kind in helping us those tyrannising days.
We thank the other counties too, that have been doing
     the same,
For every man who hears this song will know we're not
     to blame."

31. The Miners' Lock-Out in Lancashire, 1893

[*THE song "The Miners' Lock-out" was written by Burnett O'Brien, a Wigan collier, during the great lock-out of 1893 and was sung round many of the towns of Lancashire by the colliers during their collections to assist their starving children. Songs such as this were sung at Walkden by Thomas Halliday to crowds of thousands:*]

THE MINERS' LOCK-OUT

Written and composed by Burnett O'Brien, Wigan.

UNITED WE STAND — DIVIDED WE FALL

Air: Castles in the Air

"Ye gallant lads of Lancashire,
Come listen unto me —
I will unfold a tale of woe
That's very sad to see.
Our children they are starving,
You can see them day by day;
The offspring of our collier lads
For food they have to pray.

Chorus: Then let us be united
We never must give way.
Uphold the federation, lads,
And we will win the day.

It's very hard on us poor lads
That we must go away
To beg for our maintenance —
We do it day by day.
But 'tis better far to do it
Than that we should engage
To go and take our shirts off
And work for a pauper's wage.

But we must keep our tempers!
Don't let our hearts go down,
We are getting well supported
By the people of our town.
The Publicans and Tradesmen
Throw in their little mite;
They are working well on our behalf,
They know we're in the right.

We must thank our trusty leaders
They're well worthy of their steel;
The masters have not done what's right,
The hunger they don't feel.
They have found their opportunity,
It was not hard to seek;
We'd nothing — (obliterated) —
Now we must put on the check.

All honour to Sam Woods, my lads,
He's doing all he can —
Trying to get an honest wage
For the British working man.
The day is fast approaching,
When victory we will shout,
And we'll remember those who helped us
When we were all locked out.

The Miners' Lock-Out in Lancashire, 1893

Don't forget the collier lads
That are trying with their might —
Enduring so much suffering
To get that which is right;
And when you see his box displayed,
No matter where he'll roam,
Think of his wife and children
Who are starving in their home.

Chorus: Then let us be united,
We never must give way;
Uphold the Federation lads,
And we will win the day."

32. Taff Vale Railway, 1900

[THE *Taff Vale Case arose out of a local dispute. At a time when railway trade-unionism was almost wholly unrecognised by the owners, the railwaymen of the Taff Vale Railway Company in South Wales came out on strike. The company decided to proceed against the union. Its actions were successful and the company received £23,000 in damages from the Society. This judgment struck at the essential basis of all strike activity. The right to strike itself was jeopardised. The unions began nation-wide agitation against the decision that trade-union funds could be made liable for damages caused by a trade dispute. This agitation led to the winning of a large number of seats by the Labour Party in the General Election of 1906, and to the passing of the Trade Disputes Act (1906) which remedied the grievance.*]

STRIKE !

ON THE

Taff Vale Railway.

Men's Headquarters,
Cobourn Street,
Cathays.

There has been a strike on the Taff Vale Railway since Monday last. The Management are using every means to decoy men here who they employ for the purpose of black-legging the men on strike.

Drivers, Firemen, Guards, Brakesmen, and SIGNALMEN, are all out.

Are you willing to be known as a

Blackleg ?

If you accept employment on the Taff Vale, that is what you will be known by. On arriving at Cardiff, call at the above address, where you can get information and assistance.

RICHARD BELL,

General Secretary.

33. Tonypandy, 1910

"THE trouble began over the price list for a new seam in the Ely pit of the Naval Colliery Company. The owners offered a piece rate of 1s. 9d. a ton (plus 1d. for dealing with stone) while the workmen, on the ground that it was a particularly difficult seam bound to cause many abnormal places, asked for 2s. 6d. a ton. The haggling over the price went on for a long time, until the owners felt they could wait no longer and decided to force the issue by resorting to a lock-out. On September 1, 1910, they locked-out not only the few dozen who were in dispute with them but the whole eight hundred of the Ely pit, so as to bring pressure to bear on the seventy men to settle on a price that would be satisfactory to the owners. A lock-out of this kind roused resentment in the Rhondda and other valleys: and, by a ballot of the coal-field, the South Wales Miners' Federation called out on strike the whole of the twelve thousand men employed by the Cambrian Combine in the endeavour "to teach that particular company that tyrannical action over certain men to influence others was not a paying policy." The strike notices were handed in on October 1st and by November 1st the Cambrian Combine strike had begun.

Strikes also began in the Aberdare Valley, where the workmen were demanding the remedy of numerous grievances, especially those connected with abnormal places. Other strikes took place in Ogmore Valley. A state of tension began to develop throughout the coal-field. By the end of the first week in November there were 12,000 miners idle in the Rhondda Valley and 11,000 in Aberdare Valley. By mid-winter there were some 30,000 locked out or on strike.

Some South Wales coal-owners were possessed by a hope that the place of the strikers would be filled by blackleg labour. On the other side, all miners were fully aware that the Trade Disputes Act of 1906 had restored the right of "peaceful picketing." A clash between these two could be foreseen. The owners placed their trust in the Chief Constable of Glamorgan. Captain Lindsay had several score of foot and mounted police available for the two valleys, apart from the local constables; after consultation with the local magistrates (some of whom were directors or shareholders in colliery companies) he augmented this force by extra police from the cities of South Wales and from Bristol.

By Sunday, November 6th, the workmen discovered that it was the intention of the owners to import blackleg labour for the Glamorgan Colliery at Llwynpia. On the night of Monday, November 7th, a body of strikers surrounded the colliery, and had a sharp brush with a body of police ensconced in the colliery premises. Reinforcements of police were rapidly sent into the valley, where their arrival aroused resentment, especially in Tonypandy, a mile or two down the valley from Llwynpia. Between midnight and 1 a.m. on the morning of November 8th, disturbances broke out with a certain amount of smashing of windows. The police used their truncheons freely and dispersed the miners. While all this was going on, the Chief Constable of Glamorgan telegraphed to Shrewsbury, Chester and Salisbury Plain for troops and a few hours later followed up telegraphic messages to the Home Office by an urgent personal telephone call to Winston Churchill, then Home Secretary. At this point Tonypandy, from a local disturbance, became a focus of national attention and the subject of conferences at the Home Office, discussions with the War Office, questions and debates in Parliament."

R. PAGE ARNOT, *The Miners: Years of Struggle* (1953)

[*General Sir Nevil Macready was chosen by the Home Secretary, Mr. Winston Churchill, to command the troops being despatched to the area. Here is his own description of what he found:*]

"On my arrival at Pontypridd, on the evening of the 8th November, the situation was roughly as follows. The whole of the colliers of the Cambrian Combine were out on strike, and attacks had been made on certain mines to compel the officials and stokers to leave work, resulting in serious rioting on the 8th at Llwynpia, where Captain Lindsay, the Chief Constable, was besieged and could not get out, also at Tonypandy . . .

At Cardiff I was met by various military and police officials who struck me as being unduly perturbed by the reports that were coming from Tonypandy. It was pouring with rain, I had no Staff officer or even servant with me, and the few officials I managed to get in touch with at Pontypridd seemed to have lost all sense of proportion, and to be obsessed with but one idea: to flood the valleys with troops . . .

During the day I had satisfied myself that the situation, though still dangerous, had been exaggerated both by the mine owners and by the magistrates of the district. The strikers were in a bad mood, many of them specially inflamed against Mr. Llewellyn and the son of Mr. Hann, the manager of the Aberdare mines . . .

On the one side was Leonard Llewellyn, a forceful autocratic man, admired by the miners for his sporting instincts and gallantry whenever a disaster took place in one of his mines, but a man who, by his rough-and-ready methods, was apt to drive those working for him to a state of desperation. Behind him was Mr. D. A. Thomas,* who, from the dealings I had with him seemed to be under the impression that his standing as a member of Parliament gave him the right to lay down the law on any matter in which his interests were concerned. In the Aberdare Valley a Mr. Hann who controlled the employers' interests was not unpopular with the miners, having little of the overbearing manner of his brother-manager in the Rhondda Valley, but was not overblessed with physical courage. The bugbear of the miners in this part of the coal-field was a son of Mr. Hann, who had managed to incur their bitter hatred.

On the men's side the usual committees, so dear to the present-day working-classes, directed activities in both valleys . . .

* David Alfred Thomas, 1st Baron and Viscount Rhondda of Llanwern (1856-1918). M.P. for Merthyr Burghs, 1888-1910; for Cardiff, 1910-1916. Managing Director of Cambrian Combine Collieries.

In the Rhondda Valley the strike committee consisted of half a dozen fanatical socialists, strongly impregnated with the theories of Karl Marx. On several occasions they came to see me. Sparing of words as a rule, rigid teetotallers, unable to see beyond the narrow tenets of their creed, they undoubtedly exercised a strong hold over the strikers, and defied the authority of the miners' agents, the elected representatives of the men, a fact which complicated the situation as the employers very properly refused to recognize these self-constituted leaders. For my own information I made inquiries about the antecedents of the members of the strike committees, and found that as a rule they were indifferent workmen and generally without any stake in the locality. Their energies being exhausted in attending meetings and in organizing their adherents, it is hardly to be wondered that they had little time or inclination to become efficient workmen.

A curious point was that the older men, mostly married and with houses of their own, allowed themselves to be brought to the brink of destitution by men for whom they did not conceal their contempt. As the strike progressed, and times became very hard for the men, many of whom were raising money on their houses and other belongings, I often heard grumbling against the action of the strike committee, and on asking why such men were allowed to obtain such commanding influence invariably received the same answer, viz., that the older men and good workmen could not be bothered after a day's work to attend meetings and listen to the outpourings of men for whom they had little respect, and in whom they felt no confidence. As a consequence, when voting took place to fill positions in the various "lodges" the results were decided by the votes of young and irresponsible men, who had little or no stake to lose when trouble came. In justice to the strike committee in the Rhondda Valley I must say that when they gave their word to me to carry out any undertaking it was scrupulously adhered to, a line of conduct which the employers might well have imitated.

There was no difficulty in obtaining the point of view of the employers, for I had not been many hours in the locality before I was inundated with information and advice as to what I should do, all tending towards one conclusion, viz., that the employers were entirely blameless for what was occurring, and that the men should be coerced into submission by force. To find out the other side of the picture was more difficult, the strike committees having made up their minds that both police and soldiers were at the beck and call of the owners.

Thanks to the tact and astuteness of Captain Childs, a private meeting with the Rhondda strike committee was arranged, and over tea and ginger beer I managed to get a fair idea of their line of country. After I had pointed out that the cause of dispute between them and the owners was a matter of the most profound indifference to me, and that I was only there to prevent damage to property or molestation of individuals on either side, so far as the means at my disposal admitted, they seemed to thaw somewhat. Of course there was the usual wild talk, so dear to the small demagogue, one individual, Burton by name, thumping the table and asseverating that the mines would be drowned with blood if he was interfered with. Knowing that this individual had the reputation of being well to the rear whenever any rioting was in progress, I suggested that in that case no doubt he would take the first plunge into a mine, which left him mumbling for the rest of the interview.

The committee were as vehement against the misdeeds of the owners as the owners had been against the strikers. One of their main grievances was the importation of "blacklegs," which they affirmed was often done merely to irritate the men. They hinted that while they and their families were starving, I and the officers of the troops would be drinking champagne at the owners' expense, and were somewhat surprised when I told them that I had informed my officers that I did not wish them to accept any hospitality, because it must needs be one-sided and liable to misinterpretation. Before the committee left my room I told them that in order to avoid unnecessary conflict they had better keep in touch with me through Captain Childs, an arrangement which worked admirably throughout the strike, and provided me with information from time to time that went far to counter excesses which might have broken out.

A meeting with the directors of the colliers was not so satisfactory, owing to the somewhat dictatorial tone adopted by those present. The idea seemed prevalent among them that the military and police were at their disposal, to be increased to any extent they might demand, and to be allocated according to their advice. I had to point out that the numbers were dependent on what the Government might consider necessary and find available, and that the decision and responsibility for the distribution both of police and military rested with me . . .

The inclination on the part of the colliery managers to send in highly coloured and alarmist reports on account of which police and troops might have been needlessly rushed about the country became so prevalent that I had arranged for selected military officers to be stationed at the principal centres, who would pass on information or requests from managers after verifying the fact, an arrangement which had a calming effect throughout the district. Countless cases in my experience could be given to illustrate the need for such a course, which I recommend to all officers, police or military, who may be engaged on duties for the suppression of disorder in the future . . .

From a long and varied experience I have found that when disturbances have occurred, or are likely to occur, the civilian mind is apt to magnify the importance of insignificant happenings without verifying the facts or taking count of the source or nature of the information. Cabinet Ministers are particularly liable to run away with first impressions on such occasions. When such unnecessary excitements only affect Government officials not much harm is done beyond increased nerve strain, but when police or the forces of the Crown may be involved, every sudden and unnecessary move involves discomfort, wear and tear, and finally grumbling and want of confidence in their superiors . . .

. . . The golden rule that the soldiers were not to come into play until the police had exhausted all their resources was rigorously adhered to, and owing to the large numbers of police who had been drafted into the district the military rarely came into contact with the mob. In the Tonypandy Valley, however, the rioters found that the police with their heavy greatcoats and somewhat robust physique were handicapped when following agile young stone-throwers up the steep tracks that ascend the hill-side at right angles to the main road in the valley.

During the rioting that occurred on 21st November throughout the Tonypandy Valley the Metropolitan Police while driving the mob before them along the main road were heavily stoned from the side tracks, and suffered severe casualties. In order to counter these tactics on the part of the strikers on the next occasion when trouble was afoot, small bodies of infantry on the higher ground, keeping level with the police on the main road, moved slowly down the side tracks, and by a little gentle persuasion with the bayonet drove the stone-throwers into the arms of the police on the lower road. The effect was excellent; no casualties were reported, though it was rumoured that many young men of the valley found that sitting down was accompanied with a certain amount of dis-comfort for several days. As a general instruction the soldiers had been warned that if obliged to use their bayonets they should only be applied to that portion of the body traditionally held by trainers of youth to be reserved for punishment . . ."

SIR NEVIL MACREADY, *Annals of an Active Life* (1924)

34. The Dock Strike of 1911

"IT JUST grew out of despair, the very madness of despair: almost hysterically the human cry of protest broke out. We smothered it for a month, we "leaders," we "dictators," for we had not realised the hot resentment and stubborn determination of the men.

The employers scoffed at our exasperation. We simply told the men what the employers thought of them. The men grew restive, then angry, and then the thought came to them like an inspiration: they would no longer labour. Sulkily, by scores of thousands, they left their work. The work stopped — dead. Milk, ice, eggs, meat, vegetables, fruit, all manner of foods and necessaries lay there, out of the public reach. The stream of London's food supplies was stopped . . .

How often and with what a haughty unctuousness it had been demonstrated to Park Lane, and Change Alley, and Stockwell Park, and the New Cut, and the Mile End Road that Labour was dependent upon Capital; that the iron law of wages was as immutable as the force of gravity, and that the great and gifted captains of Industry made the wheels go round. And the clock stopped; and the Captains of Industry could not set it going, but sat supine and sulky, looking exceedingly foolish. Labour had said "No." Labour had put its "No" into action, and the immutable laws of economics were as futile as the empty barrows, the unfired engines, and the moveless cranes along the blank sides of the deserted docks . . .

"Mob law in London! Police helpless! Government impotent! Demagogues as dictators! Wolf at our doors! Men compelled to leave their honest toil! Sufferings of the poor! Reign of terror! Where are the respectable leaders of Labour? Where is the Cabinet? Where are the troops?" Heaven in its mercy leaves us always the Press in all our afflictions.

137

But the action of the Press is typical. The Press might scold, and rant and sneer; but the Press wanted paper! What would the world do without its half-penny oracles? What could the oracles do without paper? What would the advertiser say? The Press swanked and blustered and bluffed; but the Press did not go to the Government, nor to the troops, nor to the captains of industry for its paper; it went to the Strike committee of the working men. The Press, being a thing of wind and words, understood that wind and words will not lift and load and carry tons of paper reels: that must be done by hands: common, hard, vulgar hands. So the Press ambled off to Tower Hill, and craved permission of Mob law. It was a lesson: it was a take down. It was, as the Press too well perceived, a portent. The Press swallowed the dose, but did not like it: made the most damnable faces, said rude words about the paid agitator, and the tyrannical Sansculotte, lording it on Tower Hill. But the Press had felt a draught.

A hard world, my masters, but we demagogues manage to live in it; and to live virilly, pugnaciously, agitating, and winning; to the disgusted amazement of hireling slanderers and refined futilities.

But the fight's the thing: the strike.

The history of it is interesting. We started our organisation a year ago in Copenhagen: we licked it into shape about six months ago in London by the formation of the National Transport Workers' Federation. The dead-heads and the wailers said it was impossible; but they came along: muttering failure. The transport workers' unions took up the idea, paid their fees, claimed a share in the deliberations, and then we sprung the claim of the docker for 8d. an hour by day and 1s. an hour by night on the astounded employers. The calm ones said: "No precipitation"; the precipitators said: "No calm"; and in the hurry the calm ones got hustled along. The first sensations were irritating, then they began to like the hurry, and then they hurried, and did as well as though born hustlers.

The dockers stopped work, hardly knowing why, although we had asked them to remain in until we were able to let them know the exact position.

Then the coalies stopped. After them came the most sedate lot, the bargemen; then the lumpers, granary workers; at last the carmen and the stevedores. The railway carters thought of being able to make a fight as well.

The Press people, as I have said, came along to the Strike Committee asking the "powers that be" for authority to move paper, to distribute the printed matter. Even the Government sought the aid of the Committee; and Tower Hill became for the time being the hub of the Universe. Heads have gone off before on the same spot — now, according to the enemy, the men were off their heads. Puzzle the matter out, dear readers.

The dockers (ship-workers) got the first big advance, although the Port of London Authority had granted 1d. an hour increase before; then the coalies, then the carmen, and afterwards the lightermen. The permanent men of the docks had come out, and so it was thought advisable not to return to work unless reinstatement were assured. That got, with the lighterman's trouble over for the time being, all was plain sailing, and there was a chance to settle, and we did; and the big fight ended.

It is good to be able to chronicle these things; they are history making. Lightermen had worked day and night, carmen had worked from 5 a.m. to midnight, dockers had waited from midnight to midnight for work, expectant every minute of the possibility of labour, and the employers found delight in the thought that "men are dirt cheap"; then the coalies thought they would stand by, and so the engines stood still, and the machinery "wouldn't go," and the ships couldn't move. The docks, the river, the streets became silent; but for revolutionary rumblings and the tramp of feet, and the hoarse shouts. Meanwhile there are organisings, meetings, careful plans developed; and then the "powers that be" sought food, fodder, coal, ice; power to release foods and clear cargoes. The markets choked with garbage, the merchants with oaths and general bad language; and the men got grimmer and hungrier. Twenty thousand dockers, six hundred stevedores, six thousand lightermen, six thousand coalies, six thousand wharf-workers, four thousand granary men, forty thousand carmen, and ten thousand others joined; there was no work for tens of thousands of others. Transport was choked, the life circulation of trade was clogged, and the impotent kings of Capital raved drivel about soldiers and prisons and gallows and guns.

It was Direct Action with a vengeance. Only the hunger of the poor made a settlement possible. But the public were frightened into hysterics over the possibility of a famine — frightened in a week — and denounced the men and the people, half of whom are famine stricken fifty-two weeks in the year.

What a lesson in economics! It ought to be made patent what this all means. Employers for the first time offered advances to their men without solicitation. Strange, but true. The fear of the democracy was in their hearts — a dread greater than the fear of God.

You have read about the strike, how we tried for a month to get the employers to reason out the position, how port after port took up the cry, how section after section won the advances long overdue.

For a month we worked incessantly. The employers met us tongue in cheek, bluffed us, vulgarly insinuated we too were bluffing. And all the while we knew the passions a great mass were seething. Then the storm broke. It shook the foundations; it flooded up to the counting houses; it swirled along the dull streets, and the hovels sent out the wail and the shout of glad resentment. Did you ever see that sinister gladness, that gloating revenge, that sardonic, almost jolly, resentment?

It is the humour of the crowd that saves us from revolution. Some day it will be a grim sort of humour, and then there will be a lot of real fighting which the soldiers cannot stop.

There has been a gain of about 20 per cent. in wages, a slight reduction in hours so far as the ordinary transport worker is concerned, but so far as the carmen are concerned the 72 hours week actually knocks off as much as 50 and 30 hours to the men, besides giving them an increase in pay.

In weather such as this the docker will think nothing of waiting all the week for a job, and will scrape the refuse-heaps of the

140

coolies for rotten rice. He will wait a week on the dock, unless he is chivied off. The carmen will doze and work mechanically, while the poor, wretched horses will work a 100, a 140 hours week: and now comes the week of 72 hours.

Dockers will average from 15s. to 30s. a week.

Carmen, ditto.

Lightermen, 25s. to 35s.

Stevedores, ditto.

Coal-porters, ditto.

It is all hazardous and arduous work (ask the amateur dockers for a testimony, and hear from the lips of the tennis labourers). There are more men killed to the thousand in transport occupations than are killed in the twenty thousand of the average trades. But we have won. The Shipping Federation suddenly discovered that £200,000,000 couldn't make the wheels go round, and so they came along and said they always wanted to be fair.

It is a great country, and there is the host of workers to be co-operated together for the purpose of more directly fighting the masters.

But we have averaged a gain of 20 per cent. on the wages. It is good: if the men stick together it will be better.

The new-born Federation is to do greater and greater things. Hurrah for the fight!"

BEN TILLETT (*The Clarion*,
18th August, 1911)

35. National Railway Strike of 1911

HOW IT BEGAN

"THE railway trouble started at Liverpool, on the Lancashire and Yorkshire line, where the porters and others came out on strike for an increase of 2/- per week. They were receiving 17/- a week. The Manchester men, of similar grades, joined their Liverpool comrades, and the strike spread to other lines. The Liverpool dockers decided not to handle goods from any of the lines where the strike was on, whereupon the ship owners of the port retaliated by a general lock-out. The railway companies affected declared they were not free to give the advance asked for by their men, because they were bound by the decisions of the Conciliation Board, set up to avert a strike in 1907, at the instance of Mr. Lloyd George, as President of the Board of Trade. During the four years of its working the Conciliation Board had proved a fresh means of harassing and terrorising the railway servants, and wages had actually decreased and conditions of service worsened under its operations. In 1907 the railway men had sought to force the railway companies to recognise their Trade Unions, and allow the Union officials to present the case of the men before the directors. This recognition, however, the directors refused to concede, and so, when the men's notices were on the point of expiring and a general railway strike seemed imminent, Mr. Lloyd George came to the rescue of the companies and succeeded in inducing the Union leaders, with Mr. Richard Bell, the General Secretary, at their head, to accept the Conciliation Board instead. By 1911, however, the men had become so incensed at the chicanery, the mean and petty artifices, the long drawn-out quibbling, and the increasing tyranny and persecution which the companies were practising against them under cover of the Conciliation Boards that they resolved to make one mighty effort to secure recognition for their Unions, and a joint meeting of the Executives of the four Unions within which the different sections of railway workers are enrolled was convened to meet at Liverpool. By this time the area of the strike on the railways was gradually being extended by the spontaneous action of bodies of men acting without the authority of their Unions. Threats of similar action were pouring in from all over the country. The strike fever had seized the railway men, and the four Executives, after a careful review of the situation, wisely decided that the psychological moment for drastic action had come. They therefore issued an ultimatum to the railway companies giving them 24 hours' notice in which to agree to recognise the Unions. This was accompanied by a declaration of war. If recognition was not conceded within the time specified then every grade of railway worker on every railway would be called out. A general railway strike would follow the refusal of recognition of the Unions . . ."

J. KEIR HARDIE, *Killing No Murder* (1911)

RAILWAYS IN CHAOS

". . . Following upon the joint meeting in Liverpool, the four general secretaries of the unions travelled to London and met the President of the Board of Trade, Mr. Sydney Buxton, at three o'clock the following day. Prior to this meeting the companies' representatives had conferred with Buxton, and the net result of the day's proceedings was summed up in a statement issued to the press at 5.30 the same afternoon. "The Government having assured the railway companies that they will give them adequate protection to enable them to carry on their services, the railway companies are prepared, even in the event of a general railway strike, to give an effective if restricted service."

The next morning (Thursday) the full joint committee of the men, having travelled from Liverpool overnight, presented themselves at the Board of Trade offices for a conference with Sydney Buxton, the Cabinet meanwhile holding a council meeting in Downing Street . . .

When the Cabinet had considered (the matter) . . . the Prime Minister, Mr. Asquith, visited the men and offered them a "Royal Commission to investigate the working of the conciliation agreement, and to report what amendments, if any, are desirable in the scheme, with a view to promote a satisfactory settlement of the grievances."

This was obviously the old parliamentary game of staving off the trouble by a prolonged inquiry in the hope that the men would settle down to work and lose their enthusiasm for a fight. Unfortunately for the Government it was too obvious, and the men refused to accept the proposal . . .

Friday morning found the railways in a state of chaos. Some stations had to be closed down at once. The men struck in thousands as they finished their shifts. In under six hours 150 telegrams were received at the A.S.R.S. head office, all bearing the same words: "Men all out."

The thousands of men whom the companies had boasted were anxious to drive their engines and carry on traffic operations in the event of a strike, the men who had been repeatedly used to prove that unrest did not exist because of their desire for jobs on the railway, could not be found. It was the most effective strike that ever occurred in this country.

On behalf of the Government, Asquith, realising that his blunt and frank opposition to the men had made matters worse instead of better, gave way to the suave and wily Lloyd George, by now Chancellor of the Exchequer. The Home Secretary, Mr. Winston Churchill, kept the Government's promise to the companies by planting troops at the stations throughout the country. The dangerous method of attempting to overawe the men by a display of armed force was openly indulged in, and it was obvious to every observer that the most repressive measures would be adopted by the authorities if the slightest excuse was given . . ."

ROWLAND KENNEY, *Men and Rails* (1913)

LLANELLY

"As showing how the troops were likely to be used to shoot men down like dogs, take what happened at Llanelly. A train was stopped by a crowd of strikers squatting down on the line in front of it. Some troops, quartered at the station, rushed up at the double, and lined up on both sides of the engine. Before they got there, however, a striker had boarded the footbridge of the engine and drawn the fire, and so the engine was effectively disabled from proceeding. But for the presence of the soldiers nothing more would have happened. Some boys and youths did pelt stones at the soldiers, and one of them was struck. Mr. Lloyd George spoke of what happened as being undoubtedly a "very great riot," and described the engine driver as lying bleeding and helpless from the violence of the mob. This, however, was all imagination without an atom of truth. The train was standing in a deep cutting, and the official story is that stones were coming in showers from both sides. Now, not one pane of glass in the carriage windows was broken, not one passenger was hurt or molested, in fact, they were looking out of the windows, no civilian was struck, no property was damaged; there was no riot. But the officer in command ordered the people to disperse; he gave them one minute in which to do so; at the end of the minute he ordered five shots to be fired which killed two men outright, and wounded four others. John Johns, one of the murdered men, was sitting on the garden wall of his own house in shirt and trousers, looking on; the other was also in his garden at the top of the railway embankment. No one has ever alleged that either of them threw stones or took any part in what little stone throwing there was. Presumably, however, they made good targets, and so were picked off. For the troops are not to fire at random. They are not to use blank cartridge, even by way of warning, they are not to fire over the heads of the people, they are not to fire at the legs of the crowd; their instructions were to make every shot tell, they were to shoot to kill. At the inquest the jury, at the suggestion of the Coroner, brought in a verdict of "justifiable homicide." But, to ease their conscience, they added a rider. It was this:—

145

"We think it would have been better if other means than giving an order to fire had been adopted by Major Stuart for that purpose of dispersing the crowd."

That rider destroys the verdict of justifiable homicide. If other means could have been tried before shooting was resorted to then the killing of the two men was felonious, and not justifiable, homicide — in other words murder. The officer, having seen the two men killed, went to the driver of the train and asked him to go on, but the driver replied either that he "could not or would not," and then, naively added Major Stuart, "seeing I could have given no more service, I withdrew my men to the station." Hours afterwards when an infuriated crowd were looting, burning, and destroying railway stock, the Major and his men remained immovable until a wagon exploded and killed another four people. His orders, he said, were "explicit." Under no circumstances was he "to allow a train to be held up." Protection of life and property forsooth! I invite all good Liberals to explain this Llanelly incident on any other grounds than those I am putting forward. The throwing of a few stones, even if one soldier be hit, does not justify the shooting of two respectable lookers-on, standing in their own backyard. It was the orders to protect blackleg labour which appeared to render that necessary.

I have already expressed my opinion of the finding of the jury. There are three degrees of homicide known to the law. There is justifiable homicide, where, for instance, one man kills another in self-defence; there is excusable homicide, where one person kills another without meaning to do so; and there is felonious homicide, which is ordinary murder. Now if, as the jury stated in their rider, it "would have been better" if other means had been tried by Major Stuart of dispersing the crowd, what happened was not "justifiable homicide." Murder is only justifiable when it is the only resort left, and the jury, by saying that other means should have been tried, rob the deed of its justifiable character. What action is contemplated to have this point sifted to the bottom I know not, but the responsibility rests with the Trade Union movement to use every process known to the law to have the question fully tested. The right to strike effectively is at stake."

J. KEIR HARDIE, *Killing No Murder* (1911)

[*This strike was settled on 19th August, 1911, when, under Government auspices, the companies agreed to meet representatives of the unions.*]

36. Incitement to Mutiny, 1912

[*WHEN Tom Mann returned to England from Australia in 1910 he launched a campaign in favour of Syndicalism and Direct Action. The paper called "The Syndicalist," produced under Tom Mann's chairmanship, reprinted a leaflet (reproduced below) for which Tom Mann was arrested and sentenced to six month's imprisonment.*]

HALT! ATTENTION!!

Open Letter to British Soldiers.

This letter to British soldiers, reprinted from *Sheldrake's Military Gazette* (Aldershot), of March 1st, 1912, is the subject of the charge against Crowsley, Guy Bowman, the Buck brothers, and Tom Mann. Read and judge for yourself. Let the voice of the PEOPLE be heard.

Men! Comrades! Brothers!

You are in the Army

So are WE. You in the Army of Destruction. We in the Industrial, or Army of Construction.

WE work at mine, mill, forge, factory, or dock, producing and transporting all the goods, clothing, stuffs, etc., which make it possible for people to live.

YOU ARE WORKING MEN'S SONS.

When WE go on Strike to better OUR lot, which is the lot also of YOUR FATHERS, MOTHERS, BROTHERS, and SISTERS, YOU are called upon by your officers to MURDER US.

DON'T DO IT!

You know how it happens always has happened.

We stand out as long as we can. Then one of our (and your) irresponsible Brothers, goaded by the sight and thought of his and his loved ones' misery and hunger, commits a crime on property. Immediately You are ordered to MURDER Us, as You did at Mitchelstown, at Featherstone, at Belfast.

Don't You know that when You are out of the colours, and become a "Civy" again, that You, like Us, may be on Strike, and You, like Us, be liable to be MURDERED by other soldiers.

BOYS, DON'T DO IT!

"THOU SHALT NOT KILL," says the Book.

DON'T FORGET THAT!

It does not say, "unless you have a uniform on."

No! MURDER IS MURDER, whether committed in the heat of anger on one who has wronged a loved one, or by pipe-clayed Tommies with a rifle.

BOYS, DON'T DO IT!

ACT THE MAN! ACT THE BROTHER ACT THE HUMAN BEING!

Property can be replaced! Human life, never.

The Idle Rich Class, who own and order you about, own and order us about also. They and their friends own the land and means of life of Britain.

YOU DON'T. WE DON'T.

When WE kick, they order YOU to MURDER Us.

When You kick, You get courtmartialled and cells.

YOUR fight is OUR fight. Instead of fighting AGAINST each other, WE should be fighting with each other.

Out of OUR loins, OUR lives, OUR homes, You came.

Don't disgrace YOUR PARENTS, YOUR CLASS, by being the willing tools any longer of the MASTER CLASS.

You, like Us, are of the SLAVE CLASS. When WE rise, You rise; when WE fall, even by your bullets, YE fall also.

England with its fertile valleys and dells, its mineral resources, its sea harvests, is the heritage of ages to us.

You no doubt joined the Army out of poverty.

WE work long hours for small wages at hard work, because of OUR poverty. And both YOUR poverty and OURS arises from the fact that Britain with its resources belongs to only a few people. These few, owning Britain, own OUR jobs. Owning OUR jobs, they own OUR very LIVES.

Comrades, have WE called in vain? Think things out and refuse any longer to MURDER YOUR KINDRED. Help Us to win back BRITAIN for the BRITISH, and the WORLD for the WORKERS.

148

37. Larkinism and the Struggle in Dublin, 1913

"A DRAWN BATTLE"

[*BEFORE World War I there was so much industrial unrest in Britain that little attention was given to similar problems in Ireland. There, James Larkin, founder of the Irish Transport Workers Union, and James Connolly, militant socialist leader, began a great crusade to enrol in the Irish Transport Workers Union unorganised workers of every type and turn the union into a single and united instrument for waging war on the employers.*

After a number of successful lightning strikes followed by sympathetic strikes of other workers, employers, led by W. M. Murphy, leading proprietor of the Dublin tramways and many other enterprises, began dismissing Transport Union members and sought a signed document from their employees repudiating membership of the Union. Larkin replied by calling a General Strike of the services covered by the Transport Union. British unions soon became involved, especially when Larkin asked them not to handle goods intended for Ireland.

The strike continued through the second half of 1913. The T.U.C. through the Co-operative Wholesale Society, sent shiploads of food to the starving Dublin workers (see below) and large sums of money were collected in Britain. By January 1914, under the pressure of sheer starvation, men began to drift back to work on the employers' terms. The latter, in most cases, silently dropped "the document," and the dispute collapsed. The union, however, was not smashed and James Connolly later referred to the strike as "a drawn battle."]

THE STORY OF THE FOODSHIPS
(24th September, 1913)

"That same afternoon (the Wednesday afternoon) the deputation
was closeted with a C.W.S. buyer. An hour in his company sufficed.
What it was possible to do with their money he had put before
them; upon what was possible to be done they had agreed. Of
potatoes, 10lb.; of tinned fish, 1lb.; of sugar, 2lb.; of margarine,
¾lb.; of tea, ¼lb.; of jam, 2lb. — for each of thirty thousand lots
this was the order. Meanwhile from friendly owners a ship had been
chartered, the s.s. *Hare*. She would need to sail early on the Friday
evening for most of the packages to be distributed in good time
on the Saturday afternoon. There were forty-eight hours in
which to execute the order. Thirty thousand lots! Reckoning the
separate provision for the potatoes in each log, sixty thousand
packages! About four o'clock on the Wednesday the order came
about the ears of the departments like a whirlwind. Sugar could be
supplied; potatoes were in stock; jam was held in great quantities
at Middleton; tinned fish was to be had; and tea could be brought
from the C.W.S. department at London. But margarine was not
stocked at Balloon Street by the ton. It could be bought, but
could it be bought in time for packing? And there was the packing
itself: the bags for the potatoes, the cartons for the general
groceries, the sudden energy of labour wanted.

Telephones rang; wires were scribbled; messengers despatched;
everyone flew to action. Margarine was collected, and more
hurried down by train from the C.W.S. branch at Newcastle.
London, appealed to for the packeted tea, sent away a huge
supply that same Wednesday evening. The C.W.S. Middleton Jam
Works, as if this sort of thing happened every day, opened its
cupboards and delivered the thirty thousand 2lb. jars, sealed and
labelled, by ten o'clock on the Thursday morning. Cartons for the
packing were poured in by the C.W.S. Boxmaking Works at Long-
sight. Twenty-seven thousand C.W.S. potato bags lying at the
depot at Goole were flung across England by passenger train. It
did not matter that a Ship Canal strike had reduced imports; that

150

Jubilee caskets and seasonal fluctuations had left warehouses half empty; that the moment was unpropitious. When other resources threatened to fail, it still was possible to ask for the return of goods just previously sold to retail societies. And from this centre and from that, by rail, cart, or motor lorry, brought in triumphantly by clerks on scout duty at the stations, the foods arrived.

Biggest labour of all, the goods must be packed. Sacks upon sacks of potatoes – not less than 150 tons – needed weighing into 10lb. lots for this wholesale-retail order. Up at the potato wharf in Oldham Road, Manchester, the C.W.S. staff that had come on duty at four in the morning remained at work all that night and the day after. And still more men were wanted, and the haunts of the unemployed were scoured in vain. Word went down to the docks, and a body of fifty previous strikers marched to the relief. Loaded like hay carts, the great two-horse lorries rumbled to the Ship Canal, ten loads in twenty minutes. Over in Ireland men, women, and children were wanting food, and men's hearts went into the work. In the midst of it the Manchester dock strike was settled and the dockers returned. So the regular staff finished a forty-hour shift at nine o'clock on the Thursday night, and recommenced at five on the Friday morning.

When the rest of the great railway depot was silent, the unaccustomed work of retail packing still continued at the C.W.S. corner, by electric light under the roof and by the little moonlight in the yard beyond.

The whirlwind came upon the packing departments at Balloon Street also. Time was insufficient for pressing into service the distant resources of Pelaw and Silvertown. Upon Manchester the burden fell. Trade was good; no extra workers could be obtained. Local societies rather needed than could spare men. The regular staff buckled to the task. Scales clicked unceasingly under the mouths of hoppers; trolleys rumbled to and from the lifts; men staggered along under piles of sugar packets; there was packing and hammering and trucking, and out went the cases and down to the docks at the rate of a thousand packets an hour. Cartons by the five thousand were all insufficient, and the girls of the warehouse set themselves to the tedious and unusual task of wrapping and tying the parcels. All through the night of the Thursday the men worked on. The C.W.S. dining-room, which had provided tea for one hundred and fifty workers, gave supper and breakfast to fifty. At midnight there was a halt. The men elected their chairman, found a pianist, and sang everything they knew from hymns to ragtime songs. At four in the morning there were sandwiches and tea; at six-thirty a douche of cold water sufficed. That all this work followed the pressure of packing Jubilee caskets was of no consequence. Over in Dublin men were fighting a workers' battle, and women and children were beset by hunger. Said this employee and that: "I'll be content with what the Committee give me for this, so what it is."

The dockers broke their strike to unload the *Hare* and free her for this new cargo. Steadily and quietly the ship was filled. Very soon after five o'clock in the afternoon of Friday the 26th, there were parcels on board enough to give a complete and equal ration to each of twenty-five thousand applicants. One hundred thousand people would be assured of food for a few days at least. People gathered by the dock side; labour leaders came and went; ropes were cast off; the propeller moved; the vessel of cheer and hope was on its way to Dublin. Men clustered at the side of steamers to hail our passing; on the roof of a weaving-shed a cotton worker stood to wave Godspeed. Sirens sounded from this dock and that; clerks flattened their faces against office windows and waved their handkerchiefs; workers clustered in groups, cheering and waving wherever a works gave a point of vantage. There were cheers at Trafford Bridge and from the C.W.S. shed and the Sun Mills; out of the mist the cheers came in volleys, or in a continuous fire: "Send her along!" "Send her along!" "Hurry up!" "Be quick!" and "Good luck to you!"

In the still and misty night all outlines seemed ghostly, yet human voices made them real. At Partington it was dark, but by the sudden cheers and the loud beating upon the iron sides of the ships we knew ourselves to be seen. Thicker and thicker came the drizzling murk, yet still the deck lights shone comfortably upon well-packed cases.

Compelled to travel unhastily, it was eleven o'clock when we came to the gates of the canal at Eastham, only to lie there helpless. Beyond, in the darkness, the ebb tide was running swiftly in the narrow channel, a peril to navigation on a night like this. Midnight, and the crew and passengers began to despair of moving. After twelve o'clock a group of seamen sat to discuss the Dublin "war." Suddenly a blast of the siren. The men sprang away; bells rang; chains clanked; the great gates slowly opened. Alone, the *Hare* passed from the lock into darkness. With nine men peering into a fog impenetrable at two-ships' lengths ahead, with the siren hooting and the bells of anchored ships responding, with stolen moments of speed and instant checks and halts, the boat felt her way down a dozen perilous miles of river, between sand banks to the bar, and out to sea. "I've seen her tied up many a lighter night," said the oldest seaman aboard.

The grey morning light showed Anglesey falling astern, and an open road to Dublin. But the tide flowed against us. The stokers sweated to keep the fires clean and hot and a full head of steam; nevertheless the hours slipped away on that long passage. Noonday gleamed through the mist, and thrushes and finches settled on the boat, and then she was dressed with bunting. The pennon of the *Hare* flew, and the flag of the C.W.S., while the smoke of eagerness poured from the funnel. And at last the Irish coast loomed ahead. A workaday dredger putting to sea gave the first salute. Then the lighthouse on the Head of Howth raised its flag; and, while the *Hare* responded, Dublin and its few factory chimneys drew nearer. Soon we were in the river, and Dublin knew us for a reality. A tug by the electric power stations roused the harbour with a prolonged and joyous hooting. Then ship vied with ship, and the cheers of crews overpowered the ships' bells. Cries of blessing and "God save Larkin" came from the walls of the narrowing river, and children ran to the point of the wall where the crowd stood in a dark line to receive us. There we came to the quayside, and men flung up their right hands, and waved their caps, and shouted welcomes. For six or seven hours, from six or seven o'clock until now, this crowd had waited through mist and rain. Employers and shopkeepers had scoffed at the "food ship"; it was all a deceit; it was impossible. And hour had followed hour without result, and men had begun to wonder if they had been tricked; and the crowd had dwindled, some going home, and many more to look for strike pay at Liberty Hall. But now at last it was proved no delusion; the ship had come in. The ship! The ship! The long-expected *Hare!* the blessed food ship!

From all sides men hurried to this distant quay.

A hundred men were there to keep order; a hundred more to unload the boat. Quickly the first cases of the cargo were raced across the cleared space and into the shed for distribution. Already within this long, low shed a hill of bread had been raised. There were the 12,000 loaves which the Dublin Industrial Co-operative Society and the United Co-operative Baking Society of Belfast had supplied early that morning. To the Dublin Society, no less than to the C.W.S., belonged a part in this achievement. It was an overdraft from the C.W.S. which had enabled the Dublin Society to build the bakery that now could render such service. But it was the Dublin Society alone which gathered together a special staff of bakers at two o'clock on the Thursday morning, and kept the ovens hot right through until Saturday, and found sufficient yeast for its unusual extra baking.

Presently huge stacks of provisions were unpacked and stacked within the shed. Drapers' assistants, released by their Saturday half-holiday, took up the places for which they had volunteered; the crowd outside was drilled by its Napoleonic leader into a queue hundreds of yards long; and the procession of resolute poor filed through the shed. Burdened with the triple gift of potatoes, groceries, and bread, and wanting a third hand for biscuits given by the C.W.S. Crumpsall Works as an addition, they passed outside to discover and arrange the treasure. And then, and only then, did the fullness of the provision begin to be realised. Tea, sugar, and jam; tinned salmon in this parcel, tinned herrings and tomato in that.

"And all so nicely packed!" "A credit to them and to all that sent it!"

Yet even then there waited a further discovery. In houses where "raspberry and apple" bought "round the corner" had been thrown away as bad, the eager children found under the Middleton cover a little label inviting the return of the jam if unsatisfactory. It was the final touch. These were no scraps and broken bits. The gift was of the best, and as from their fellows. "Ah, now," said one man, proudly (he had not eaten for twenty-four hours), "it's themselves might be wanting our help some day."

So the miracle came to Dublin. Until two in the morning people sat in the streets talking of the day. The 20lb. potato bags, too large for their own contents, beautifully had held the entire provision. Since the bags bore the C.W.S. imprint and were in demand, half-pennies had been offered for the return of them by children. But not for shillings would their new owners part with them.

"Larkin did it," the people said (that was inevitable), but co-operation was remembered also. "Dublin men are all asleep not to have a big co-operative store of their own." A tremendous cheer for co-operation echoed across the Liffey from the meeting on the Sunday afternoon. For it was realised that the food ship had come not from trade unionism alone, but from a great, common effort of the people."

PERCY REDFERN, *The Wheatsheaf*
(November 1913)

38. Strikes in World War I

[*WHEN war broke out in 1914 the majority of trade union leaders gave support to the Government and the traditional socialist opposition to war largely collapsed. Only a left-wing minority in the I.L.P. and the British Socialist Party opposed the war. Since a virtual industrial truce had been proclaimed any strike action had to be "unofficial." In 1914, the railwaymen successfully negotiated a "war bonus" with the railway companies, but this was not extended to other trades. In February, 1915, when the army was perilously short of ammunition, the whole country was startled by a great unofficial strike of engineering workers on the Clyde, one of the most important armament producing areas. This was only settled after Government intervention which granted a somewhat larger advance than the employers had offered. In March, 1915, the* Munitions of War Act, 1915, *was passed which made compulsory arbitration, as well as the suspension of Trade Union customs and the limitation of profits in munitions, legally enforceable.*]

REVOLT ON THE CLYDE

"By the evening all the principal factories had decided. The great Clyde Strike of February 1915 was on.

The strike was, and still is, wrongly referred to as an "unofficial" strike. Such a term is entirely misleading. Branch officials, district officials and in some cases, executive officials (like myself) were involved. The more correct term for such a strike is "spontaneous strike." Such strikes have played an important part in the development of the trade union movement and are often recognized and supported by the national officials. Such a strike is necessary when something occurs, leaving only the option of submitting or fighting. It may be the introduction of a non-unionist, where trade union membership is insisted on by the union as a condition of employment. It may be a cut in a recognized rate or, as was the case at Weir's, the introduction of privileged workers from outside at the expense of Weir's own employees.

If ever there was a "spontaneous" strike that called for the support of the national officials, this was the one. We had no objection to American engineers or any others getting jobs; we had no objection to their getting high wages, but we certainly did object, as trade unionists ought to object, to working ourselves at the same job for lower wages.

At the St. Mungo Hall meeting we decided to hold mass meetings in all the areas round the principal factories the following morning and to send in the afternoon a representative from each area to a meeting at which a Central Strike Committee would be formed.

These mass meetings were tremendous and gave everyone a great feeling of power. The representatives met in the afternoon at the Herald League Bookshop, George Street, which was run by an old comrade, W. McGill, and his wife, and was the headquarters of a semi-anarchist group associated with the *Weekly Herald*.

In order to escape the threats of the Defence of the Realm Act, we formed, instead of a "Strike" Committee, a "Labour-With-holding" Committee, with myself as chairman and J. M. Messer as secretary. At our first meeting we had to take note of the fact that the Government had hurriedly called together the national officials of the bigger unions and had given them their instructions — "Call off this strike."

Representatives of the national committees rushed to Glasgow and did their utmost to break the strike. But they got a rough reception. What a spectacle they presented! Not an argument of any kind against the strike; intimidated by the Government, they were merely maudlin in their pleading to us to give it up.

An old friend of mine, who had gone to work with me for many years, and had later been elected from the area to the A.S.E. executive, said to some of us: "It's all right for you fellows, but we've been called up by the Government and, while they were

157

very suave and courteous, we could feel the threat behind all they said."

"What threat?" we asked.

"The threat of imprisonment," he replied.

"Who for?"

"For us," he moaned.

Did we laugh! We were like the absentee Irish landlord who refused to be intimidated by threats against the life of his bailiff. Old "Sanny" got no sympathy from us.

The *Glasgow Herald* of Friday, February 19, reported a meeting at the Palace Theatre, in the south side of Glasgow, at which Brownlie, Gorman and Burton, from the Executive Committee of the A.S.E. were present. The reports reads as follows:

"The men were very adverse in their criticism of the Executive Council and interrupted Mr. Brownlie a good deal when he attempted to persuade them to act on the advice of their council and resume work. One of the other Council members they declined to hear. In the end they passed a unanimous resolution in favour of remaining idle until the advance of 2d. per hour was granted."

But I do not think it would be possible now to get anything like an understanding of the atmosphere which surrounded this great strike. All over the country the Press, platform and pulpit had been used to whip up a frenzy of hate. War-fever was spreading like an evil plague. Atrocity stories and propaganda lies of every kind were being served out and eagerly taken up. Anyone who dared to raise his voice in protest was a "pro-German," if not an actual hired agent of the enemy. Into the midst of all this madness, all these lies and hypocrisy, burst the strike on the Clyde. What a roar of rage went up from the war-makers! The Press shrieked for action against the leaders; everywhere in the ranks of the bourgeoisie and petty-bourgeoisie we were cursed and condemned. Of all the multitude of Press organs, with the exception of one or two weeklies with very small circulations, there was not one to say a word for us."

WILLIAM GALLACHER, *Revolt on the Clyde*
(1936)

158

39. Munitions of War Act, 1915

". . . IF ANYTHING was calculated to fray the temper of the workers and to fan their sullen resentment into open revolt it was the Munitions of War Act (July 1915) . . . Under the Act it became a penal offence to leave without the consent of the employer. It was a penal offence to refuse to undertake a new job however low the wage rate or piece rate. To refuse to work over-time whether extra time was paid or not was an offence. A worker could not leave, even after giving notice, to go from one Munitions shop to another, however low his wages might be. On the other hand the employer was not bound to give work or wages. Men were told to stand-by waiting for materials, losing hours and days, but employers refused to give leaving certificates without which no one could employ the worker. Before the Munitions Tribunal 60 to 70 cases were being heard every day of the week. The Chairman of the Tribunal could pronounce a sentence against which there was no appeal.

Such restrictions upon industrial labour rights and personal liberties were in flagrant contradiction to the traditional rights of the working class movement, and demanded sacrifices for a war which the militant trade unionists and socialists looked upon as a struggle between rival imperialist groups merely for territory and trade.

The unofficial movement which had died down somewhat after the Engineers' (February) Strike began to regather strength. It received a new impetus from the arrest of one of the militants in Parkhead Forge. This was the Marshall case. An engineer named Marshall had struck a non-union man in the jaw and laid him out. It was, to say the most of it, a case of assault. But the utmost use was made by the prosecution of the cry of "slacking" and "ca' canny" and Marshall was sentenced to three months' imprisonment. Funds were raised for the support of Marshall's family, and preparations were being made for a strike when he was liberated.

From this moment steps were taken to enlarge the Unofficial Committee, which had so far been confined to engineering and shipbuilding workers. Now railwaymen and miners were included. Very soon another case was to bring fresh confidence to the reviving mass movement. This was the Fairfield case.

One day in October 1915, one of the managers in Fairfield Works saw one or two shipwrights standing-by, waiting to get work. He ordered the dismissal of two men. They were given their clearance certificate, but the reasons for dismissal were clearly marked on them. This was the old hated "Document," which the Trade Unionists of a generation back had fought to abolish. A strike occurred in support of the two men. Seventeen men were brought before the Munitions Tribunal and fined £10 each or one month in prison. Fourteen of the men paid the fine, but three of the seventeen refused to pay on principle. They were socialists. They preferred to go to prison for a month, as they rightly believed that the payment of the fine implied recognition of the Acts, and admission that they were criminals. There began immediately a great movement for their release.

The Govan Trades Council issued explanatory circulars and forms of resolution of protest. Eventually a large delegate meeting took place representing some 97,000 workers. From this meeting an ultimatum was sent to the Government that if the men were not released in three days there would be a stoppage of work. The next day it was announced that the men's fines were paid. But by whom? Certainly not by the men or any of their friends. It was suspected then that either the officials of the Trade Unions had paid them, or the government had ordered the release of the men or there had been collusion of officials and government.

The cumulative effects of the rising cost of living contrasted with the profiteering going on, the restrictions and punitive measures imposed upon the workers by the Munitions Acts and the Defence of the Realm Act, coupled with the handing away of the powers of the Trade Union Executives under the Treasury

Agreement, was by this time crystallising into deep widespread unrest and into direct action by the workers."

TOM BELL, *John Maclean, a Fighter for Freedom* (1944)

40. The War and the Engineers, 1916

"THE case of a young engineer named Hargreaves brought us a new crisis. He happened to work in the same department as myself. After he had been absent from work for a few days it became known that he had been taken into the army, despite his possession of badge and certificate of exemption.

Had he been taken into some section of the army to work as a skilled worker where his skill as an engineer would have been of some use, perhaps the feeling would not have been so great, at least it would not have been so clear a case of victimisation.

It was reported to the shop stewards and the news passed through the workshops like wildfire. It was reported to the trade union branches, to the District Committee, to the other unions of skilled workers, to the Trade Union Executives. Weeks went by and nothing happened. More calling up notices were being received. Finally the District Committee of the A.S.E. decided to call a mass meeting in one of the local picture theatres, 'The Coliseum.' The date fixed was November 8, 1916. The skilled workers of other unions were invited to attend.

Although the Union Executives were informed of the prospective meeting a week beforehand no information was forthcoming, either with regard to Hargreaves or their intention of being represented at the meeting. There must be something in the nature of the life of a bureaucracy, whether it be of a Government, trade union, political party or a religious institution that deadens the receptive faculties and smothers the imagination. Whether it is the comfortable life of the office, the necessary routine of their work with its rules and regulations, or a cynicism engendered by their escape from industrial life, I, for the moment, leave to the sociologist and the psychologist to sort out. But the fact is that nine hundred and ninety-nine times out of a thousand a bureaucracy proves to be a first-class instrument for 'passing the buck.' So it was to prove in this case.

November the 8th arrived. Normally 'The Coliseum' seated fifteen hundred people. On this day long before the time for the meeting to begin the place was packed to the last inch of standing room and great crowds of men could not get in.

I have addressed many meetings, small and large, in the course of the years, but this was most memorable. Not because of any feat of oratory on my part, but because it was the revolt of the craftsmen and particularly the older craftsmen who saw their life's work being torn to pieces.

The President of the A.S.E. for the Sheffield and Rotherham District, Sam Armitage, was in the chair. He was an elderly man, a craftsman who from his earliest days had fought the good fight of the union and helped to build it. He had been through the lock-outs and the strikes of the union and never wavered. He announced that the District Committee had decided to suspend its meetings and hand over the business of dealing with the present issue to the Shop Stewards Committee so that the union would be free from any legal commitments that might arise in dealing with it. That did not mean he was going to hide behind legalities. He was himself a shop steward and he would be with them whatever they decided to do.

The shop stewards took charge. As most of the members of the District Committee were shop stewards it meant very little change but it facilitated the establishment of the joint leadership of the skilled unions. I reported to the meeting all that had been done about the Hargreaves case and why we had finally called this meeting.

Stanley Burgess, who was an orator, had his turn. Bill Gavigan, the District Secretary of the A.S.E., made a patriotic appeal to the men to leave the issue in the hands of the Trade Union Executives. It was then that the most stirring developments took place. Men, of long standing membership of their unions, who had lost sons in the war, who had sons at the front, spoke with a sincerity and feeling that no orator could achieve. They said 'We feel we have been betrayed and are being betrayed. We accepted the proposals of the Treasury Agreement reluctantly and because of the written pledge of the Government both as to the position of the engineers in the war and after the war. We are not unpatriotic. We have seen thousands of lads senselessly recruited for fighting when they were needed here. We have trained thousands to take their places. But if the Government is allowed to tear up its agreement now, as the German Government tore up its agreement, how can we face the lads when they come back?"

It required only a few whose losses were known to speak on these lines and it was useless for anyone to try to divert the meeting by flag waving. It was decided to give six days notice to the Trade Union Executives and the Government, that unless Hargreaves was returned to civilian life in that time and resumed his position with us under the agreement of the skilled unions with the Government, the Sheffield engineers would cease work.

The following day telegrams and letters were dispatched to these authorities.

The six days passed and all authorities ignored us. We were now put to the test. We had not been idle during the week. If there were any engineering workshops in Sheffield without shop stewards before that time there were none known to us six days after the ultimatum had been delivered. We knew what we were up against — that three-quarters of the country would be solid against us; that the employers, the military authorities and the Government would stop at nothing to crush this 'rebellion' — if they saw even a suspicion of weakness or hesitation on our side. So we took care that our plan of action was complete. All the shop stewards on the night shift were called together for four o'clock, when the ultimatum expired. They were to convey the news to the factories, inform the shop stewards on the day shift and call on the night shift to cease work. At the same time a fleet of motor cyclists which we had organised during the week were waiting outside the Engineers' Institute for the signal to go. Each cyclist had his specific route and directions. They were to go to all the important engineering centres, North, South, East and West, meet the District Committees and shop stewards wherever they went and inform them of what had happened. Other delegates were sent by train. At five p.m. that evening ten thousand engineers of Sheffield and

Rotherham walked out of the engineering factories determined that they would not return until they had won their test case.

What our correspondence had failed to do the stoppage of the men effected promptly. It was a remarkable scene when two days later the ten thousand assembled in a great meeting saw Hargreaves on the platform with the Shop Stewards committee.

So concluded a dispute which would not have occurred but for the stupidity of those in authority. Had the Ministry of Munitions and the Executive Councils of the unions, on receiving our first communications, settled the question at issue instead of debating whether the shop stewards were official or unofficial, there would have been no strike. Indeed I venture to say that from my own experience and knowledge of so-called unofficial disputes, that nine out of ten would never reach the point of strike action if those in authority dealt first with the question about which the workers are aggrieved and settled the question of prestige and dignity afterwards.

It is a false and stupid idea to think that strikes are the result of the machinations of agitators. At the heart of every strike is a deep-seated grievance of the workers involved. Workers don't throw up their jobs and face loss of wages without strike pay just for fun. Only the stupid and the ignorant think they do. But the stupid and the ignorant are in high places as well as low.

It was the offended dignity of bureaucrats which made the strike inevitable once the challenge of the military authorities had been taken up by the engineers in the workshops. The engineers won. In winning they gained confidence and became conscious of the power that was theirs, once they were organised in the workshops.

Some suspicious people will ask 'where did the shop stewards get the money from to send their emissaries all over the country?' The answer is a simple one. The stewards themselves contributed and the committee borrowed money from their workmates. Then after the strike they organised a collection in every workshop. We spent over a hundred pounds. We collected more, called a further mass meeting and presented the balance sheet and details of income and expenditure to the men. They not only approved the report but for the first time in their history as skilled workers they agreed enthusiastically to extend the method of workshop organisation to unskilled workers and women workers.

How inspiring to witness the breakdown of barriers of prejudice in the onward march of man!"

J. T. MURPHY, *New Horizons* (1941)

41. Police on Strike, 1918

"DOWNING STREET was packed from end to end with a shouting and cheering mob. The crowds overflowed into Whitehall, and from the Embankment and Trafalgar Square columns of marching men, with colourful banners fluttering in the summer breeze, were coming to swell their ranks.

This was the scene on Saturday, 31 August 1918. Number Ten Downing Street, the residence of the Prime Minister, the Right Honourable David Lloyd George, was virtually under siege by strikers and there was not a policeman in sight to restore order. Not, that is, a uniformed policeman, though soon Metropolitan and City policemen were present in force, all dressed in their Sunday best. The huge banners belonged to their own Union — the National Union of Police and Prison Officers, an organization which the Metropolitan Commissioner, Sir Edward Henry, had forbidden them to join on threat of instant dismissal.

All London now knew that its world famous Bobbies had gone on strike. Thousands of civilians, and many soldiers home on leave from France, had also gathered in Whitehall to find out for themselves what was happening. The morning papers had reported that the Prime Minister was going to meet the strike leaders himself, at midday, to discuss peace terms.

Most Londoners could not believe at first that such a strike had actually happened. Surely their good old dependable policeman, such a reassuring sight as they wished him 'Good-night' on their doorsteps and watched his measured tread along his regular beat, was not going to leave decent folk unguarded at night? It seemed a miracle that there had been no rioting already, although there were ugly but unconfirmed rumours of looting in the East End and of young women being attacked on the streets in broad daylight. Mr. Lloyd George had got to do something quickly. He should call out the soldiers, many were saying, and indeed it looked as if the Government was taking their advice, for a detachment of the Scots

167

Guards had marched from their barracks and fallen in smartly in the courtyard of New Scotland Yard. There was in the Foreign Office quadrangle facing into Downing Street even a machine gun, ominously mounted and loaded. Soldiers wearing tin hats and with bayonets fixed guarded the entrance to every government building in Whitehall.

But this was no raging, violent demonstration. Everyone was in a very good humour indeed. As Grenadier Guardsmen clambered down from their trucks in Downing Street, cheerful strikers held their rifles for them and cleared a pathway into the Foreign Office quadrangle so that the soldiers could join their colleagues who had been on duty there during the night. But reinforcements were also arriving for the strikers. The marching columns were singing as they drew near Downing Street and waving as they filed past the Home Office, where the skeleton week-end staff, suddenly reinforced by every official who could be located, stared out of the windows.

Outside Number Ten, the familiar blue uniforms had been replaced by a couple of armed soldiers, who were more than a little embarrassed to find themselves surrounded by such an unprecedented crowd. They hardly had room to execute their smart salutes as one famous figure after another elbowed his way through the onlookers to be admitted by the staff.

Those closest to the Prime Minister's house had the best view of the ministers as they hurried to the meeting. They were quick to recognize the dapper General Smuts, and they had a special cheer for Mr. Winston Churchill as he forced his way through and hurried inside. Mr. Churchill was not so universally popular after the Dardanelles disaster, but London's police still remembered him as the Home Secretary who had got them the right to one day off a week. The men were convinced that if only the present Minister, Sir George Cave, had understood their problems as well as Mr. Churchill did, there would have been no need for this strike. Where was the Home Secretary, anyway? Where was their chief, Sir Edward Henry? No one had seen either of them since the strike began.

168

Just after noon a full-throated roar of triumph broke out in Whitehall and surged through the crowd in Downing Street as a lone taxi nosed its way towards Number Ten. Out stepped Mr. Charles Duncan, MP, General Secretary of the Workers' Union and Honorary President of the Police Union. He paused on the steps and waved back to the crowd and they cheered him again.

But the cheers which came a few minutes later were even more deafening. A small group of men, soberly dressed in the unmistakable fashion of policemen out of uniform, were marching slowly up the street, and the crowd was falling back to let them through. The noise swelled and echoed from the surrounding buildings as every policeman present recognized the tall, heavily built figure of Constable James Marston, the Chairman of the Union; the man who had started the strike. Alongside Marston there marched John Crisp, the Acting Honorary Secretary, who had addressed the ultimatum to the Home Secretary and the Commissioner. With them were six other members of the Executive Committee of the Union and Tommy Thiel, the big constable from Hammersmith who had been sacked a few days before because he was the Union's provincial organizer. 'Good old Tommy,' his friends in the crowd called out, 'we won't go back to work without you!' Marston, too, paused to wave to his followers before disappearing inside. At ten minutes past twelve James Carmichael, the militant leader of the London Trades Council, the last of the strikers' representatives, arrived at Number Ten. Carmichael had been well to the fore in every strike in London and there had been plenty of those during the previous few months.

The crowd waited, the policemen among them savouring the thought that their executive, humble constables who had defied authority and dared to run a union in the force, were sitting down at the same table as the great Mr. Lloyd George. More cheers followed, but these were ironic, mocking, as at twenty past twelve an official car arrived, bearing Sir George Cave and Sir Edward Henry. Both men looked white and shaken. They hurried from the car and through the open door of Number Ten. The door closed, and the crowd settled down to await the outcome of the talks in the Cabinet Room.

To pass the time, some enterprising spirit had arranged for the best soloists from the famous Police Minstrels to lead them in community singing. So enthusiastic was their rendering of 'Goodbye Dolly' and 'Keep the Home Fires Burning' that the strains of the huge impromptu choir drifted into the room as Marston stated his case, providing a reminder of the great strength of his support. There was even a piper to add to the gaiety.

Seated in the Cabinet Room, Lloyd George, flanked by the Home Secretary and Commissioner of Police, faced the strikers' representatives across the wide table with its cut glass carafe of water and match boxes neatly placed beside each ash tray. Most of those present had never been there before yet they were more sure of themselves than the ministers they were facing. Soon after the talks started the Prime Minister was informed that the Grenadier Guards outside were fraternizing with the strikers and openly saying they would refuse to obey any order to clear them from the street.

Most of the arguments in that room during the previous four years had concerned events across the Channel where millions of men were locked in combat. Only six days before the Prime Minister had sat at this same table reading a report from his Senior Military Adviser, General Sir Henry Wilson, the Chief of the Imperial General Staff.

One paragraph of that report must have been in his mind as he listened to the strikers putting their case.

'I have no hesitation in saying that . . . we should fix the culminating period for our supreme military effort on the Western Front not later than 1st July, 1919.'

The war probably going on for at least another year; industrial unrest throughout the country; police in the capital city in a state of mutiny and in virtual control of Whitehall; the only soldiers available young recruits or sick and wounded men not looking forward to going back to the slaughter; many of them known to be sympathetic to the police claims. What could he do?

Half an hour passed; an hour. Then the front door of Number Ten was opened again. It was Carmichael. Eager hands raised him on to a wall where he could command silence. 'You've won,' he bellowed at the sea of faces below him. 'This is the greatest victory for freedom and justice that has ever been won in this country.'

They cheered, they laughed, they applauded, shook each other by the hand and slapped their neighbours on the back. Women hugged their menfolk and they all began to surge out of Downing Street to gather with the still greater crowds in Whitehall and continue the celebrations. When Marston and his committee emerged a few minutes later, they were borne on strong shoulders through the ranks of their followers, the 'Jolly Good Fellows' who had led the mutiny which no one had dreamed would take place.

Those were the cheers of men who had gambled everything and won, who knew that their livelihoods were at stake when they had obeyed the call to go on strike. Now they were going back. They had beaten Sir George Cave and, although they did not know it yet, they had destroyed Sir Edward Henry.

During those sixty minutes in the Cabinet Room, the Government had given the impression of complete surrender to the strikers. There is only one explanation and this was given by Lloyd George to a policeman in the House of Commons one evening several years later. 'This country was nearer to Bolshevism that day than at any time since.' "

GERALD W. REYNOLDS and ANTHONY JUDGE
The Night the Police went on Strike (1968)

[*In July 1919 the Police Union called another strike, but this time failed to hold its own against the Government Bill prohibiting trade unionism in the police forces.*]

42. The 40-Hour Strike, 1919

[*IN THE immediate post-war period the industrial struggle centred around the question of hours of labour. Most industries were successful in obtaining a forty-eight hours week. On the Clyde, however, joint movements, covering a number of industries, called for a general strike in favour of a forty-hour week. This strike ended in defeat, after a display of military force by the Government.*]

A GLASGOW ACCOUNT

"Here is the official appeal for strike action:

TO THE WORKERS
A CALL TO ARMS

The Joint Committee representing the official and unofficial sections of the industrial movements having taken into consideration the reports of the Shop Stewards in the various industries, hereby resolve to demand a 40-hour maximum working week for all workers, as an experiment with the object of absorbing the unemployed.

If a 40-hour week fails to give the desired results a more drastic reduction of hours will be demanded.

A general strike has been declared to take place on Monday, January 27th, and all workers are expected to respond.

By order of the Joint Committee representing all workers.

WM. SHAW
DAVID MORTON   *Joint Secretaries*

By January 28th, 100,000 workers were out. Dockers, engineers, electricians, steel workers, shipyard workers, builders, miners — the backbone of industrial Scotland — were on strike.

On Wednesday, January 29th, an enormous meeting was held in the St. Andrew's Hall, which could not cope with the crowd that turned up. Four overflow meetings had to be held. After speeches by Shinwell, Kirkwood and three London delegates, amidst great enthusiasm, the following resolution was passed:

"That this meeting pledges its support to the Joint Committee, and urges it to prosecute the strike with the utmost vigour till the Government is forced to open up negotiations with the Committee, and that when this is done the Joint Committee should submit the Government's proposals to the rank and file, with a view to a satisfactory settlement on the basis of the 40-hours' week for all time, piece and lieu workers, without any reduction of wages."

A huge procession was formed and a march began to Pinkston power station and to George Square, the centre of the city, the trams being held up *en route*. In George Square speeches were made by Shinwell, Neil Maclean and Kirkwood, and a deputation was appointed to interview the Lord Provost regarding the position of the tramways during processions, The Corporation officials at first refused all admission to the Lord Provost. Only after the personal approach of Neil Maclean and Shinwell did he agree to receive the deputation.

The Lord Provost took the opportunity to offer to make representations to the Prime Minister and Sir Robert Horne, the Minister of Labour, on the forty-hours' demand. The deputation accepted the offer, and agreed to call at the City Chambers on Friday at 12.30 p.m. to hear the answer. All the workers were invited to the Square to learn the results of the interview. We did not see, then, the subtle character of this manoeuvre to gain time and to prepare for a violent attack on the striking workers, with a view to smashing the strike. As we shall see later, the deputation didn't get the chance of having any reply from the Government. The police saw to that.

Meanwhile the strike extended. District Strike Committees were formed representing all workers in each area, regardless of their occupation or whether unemployed; whether trade unionist or not, and including housewives. These committees appointed sub-committees for organisation; propaganda and publicity; sports and entertainment; couriers, etc., and for the granting of permits to move foodstuffs. A cycle corps ran between the districts and the Central Committee, carrying reports, messages, and the strike bulletin, which was issued daily.

When the strike began, one of the first acts of the committee was to print a daily bulletin for its own purposes of publicity. Here again the Socialist Labour Press filled the breach. A group of S.L.P. comrades worked night and day, voluntarily, getting out this strike bulletin (the organ of the forty-hours' movement). Beginning with 10,000 copies we reached 20,000 daily, running two Sunday editions as well. These bulletins, a four-page sheet, were sold at a penny each and distributed by the strikers themselves. Twenty thousand was the maximum capacity of our machine or we could have sold as many more.

I recall the meeting of the joint committee, which met in the office of the Trades Council secretary, to discuss the preparations for Friday's demonstration. We had scarcely begun when the doors were burst open and a group of detectives marched into the room. They were evidently only intent on taking stock of who was who, as they contented themselves with a close scrutiny of faces, and after ordering everyone present to write his name on a piece of paper, went away.

When the police departed we got down to discussing policy. The question put was, "what were we going to do with the mass demonstration on Friday — first in the event of any further proposals or promises, and, second, should we get a flat refusal?" One proposal* was to lead the workers along the well-to-do streets and let them loose. Another proposal was to go to the houses of the bourgeois city councillors and smash in their windows. But when somebody mischievously proposed to begin with some of the Labour councillors, the idea was dropped. In the midst of the discussion two strikers came in to say that strike-breakers were being held inside

* The law of libel forbids giving the names of the movers of these two proposals. Suffice to say both of them are highly respectable Labour members of Parliament.

the Pinkston power station, food being supplied to them and beds provided; and that they (the workers) had made plans to blow the station up with dynamite. The reactions of the orthodox professional type of trade union officials present may be better imagined than described!

I argued strenuously for, and eventually we agreed on, concentrated demonstrations to be made to the various electric power stations, and such workers as were still operating, with a view to extending the strike in the city. But, alas! "the best laid plans of mice and men gang aft agley." Circumstances were to arise on Friday which were certainly not anticipated. We had made a big blunder.

According to our programme the demonstrations began to arrive from the districts, with banners, and some with bands. The Square, where the workers gathered, is a compact enclosure housing, at one end, the City Chambers; on the left the post and telegraph offices; on the right, hotels for the railway terminus for trains from the north, and at the opposite end to the City Chambers, business offices and warehouses. By twelve o'clock the Square was chock full.

From the left side of the City Chambers came the East End contingent, led by the committee and a brass band. Heading the committee was a big, burly iron-moulder. As this contingent came up the crowd made way for the band. Just as they got to the entrance to the Square and were commencing to march past the main entrance to the City Chambers, the mounted police, who formed a cordon round the entrance, blocked the way. The band and the crowd wavered for a moment. Our iron-moulder called for the band to come on. Just then one of the mounted police, by a skilful feint, tumbled his horse. This was the signal for drawing truncheons and the police began to attack right and left. A mineral water lorry, standing in a side street, was seized by the strikers and the bottles were hurled at the police. Our iron-moulder got a blow from a truncheon which laid him out for a few moments.

Meanwhile, the deputation had gone into the City Chambers to interview the Lord Provost. They were informed he was engaged at the moment. After waiting in a side room for twenty minutes they again made enquiries; still he was engaged. As a matter of fact he was consulting Sheriff Mackenzie, who was in attendance, as to the advisability of dispersing the crowd who were waiting impatiently outside. Presently an uproar was heard going on outside. The deputation now realised that they had been deceived by the Lord Provost. Shinwell and Kirkwood rushed out to restore quiet. Kirkwood was waving his arms to the crowd when he got knocked senseless with a baton, and afterwards was carried into the Council Chambers for the attention of the ambulance nurses, who were already in the building — a proof that the attack by the police was premeditated.

Gallacher, who was near by, seeing the savagery of the police, made a rush at the chief constable and gave him a terrific blow in the face. Needless to say, the chief's attendants belaboured poor Gallacher and rendered him almost unconscious. In the meantime Sheriff Mackenzie, accompanied by the Lord Provost and police officials, appeared in front of the City Chambers, and read the Riot Act. This was the signal for the police to extend their savage batoning to the crowd.

As president of our union I had to preside over Executive meetings every day, to deal with questions of policy and the holding of our members solid for the strike. We had been busy that day dealing with a district whose leading committee was not in favour of the strike, and also the question of compelling foremen and managers, who were union members, to stop work — a very important measure, since it had been the practice in the past to leave foremen and managers at work to carry on production with the aid of apprentices and labourers. When I reached the Square Gallacher and Kirkwood were standing, heads swathed in bandages, on the window balcony of the Council Chambers, exhorting the workers to go away to the Glasgow Green, and they would follow.

I learned that some of our comrades had got badly smashed, and had gone up to the S.L.P. rooms in Renfrew Street. I hurried up to see what was the extent of their injuries. Here I found Shinwell behind locked doors. We kept him there till it grew dark; got him food and arranged a disguise for him. Then I took him to a clandestine office we had for our press work. Arrangements were made to collect a responsible group of the committee to meet. At this meeting we decided on sending delegates to Belfast, and to England, to inform the workers there of the situation in Glasgow.

After the Glasgow Green demonstration was over, bands of demonstrators, on their way through the city, began to smash windows in the fashionable streets, and well into the night the police were kept busy in a form of guerrilla warfare. In the meantime military assistance was called for, and during the night troops with tanks poured into the city from the military barracks, Maryhill, and from Stirling Castle. Saturday morning found the military patrolling the streets; soldiers posted at all banks, post offices, bridges, power stations, and railway depots; while a battery of tanks and machine guns was stationed in the cattle market, Gallowgate, ready for anything.

This intimidation by military force, coupled with the fact that only a few unions officially recognised the strike and therefore most of them withheld financial assistance, decided the issue. The strike persisted for another ten days, by which time it was obviously impossible to hold out much longer, and on February 12th the strike was called off."

THOMAS BELL, *Pioneering Days* (1941)

MANIFESTO

OF THE

JOINT STRIKE COMMITTEE, GLASGOW.

A CALL TO BRITISH LABOUR.

DASTARDLY ATTEMPT TO SMASH TRADE UNIONISM.

FELLOW-WORKERS,

Ever since the Armistice was signed it has been evident that a big unemployment crisis was imminent unless steps were taken to absorb into industry the demobilised men of the Army and Navy. Thousands of these are being demobilised every day. Over a hundred thousand workers in Scotland have been dismissed from civil employment. They are out of a job. There are no jobs for them. There is only one remedy: reduce the hours of labour. The Joint Committee representing the Scottish Trades Union Congress Parliamentary Committee, the Glasgow Trades and Labour Council, and a number of other important Unions initiated the movement for a Forty Hours Week with a view to absorbing the unemployed. A strike for this object began on 27th January. This has the support of Trades Unionists all over the British Isles.

On the 29th, a huge demonstration was held and a deputation from the strikers interviewed the Lord Provost of Glasgow, who offered to appeal to the Government on the matter, and arrangements were made for another demonstration on Friday to receive the reply. On that day many thousands of strikers marched, in orderly procession, to George Square for this purpose. There was no disorder. The demonstrators were, however, met by a vicious bludgeoning attack by the police. The authorities had evidently determined to break the strike by force, and had made their plans accordingly. With such ferocity did the police make their attack that even the members of our deputation, who were there by arrangement with the Lord Provost, were attacked, and one of them—D. Kirkwood—was brutally bludgeoned from behind as he was leaving the Council Chambers. Remember that this was a peaceful and orderly demonstration of workers from all districts of

178

the Clyde area. It was met by police batons, which were used indiscriminately upon men, women and children.

Since then the authorities have imported thousands of troops into the city with machine guns and tanks for the purpose of breaking the spirit of the strikers and forcing them back to work.

On the following day the offices of the Glasgow Trades and Labour Council, the centre of Scottish Trade Unionism, were forcibly raided by the police.

Three years ago we were told by spokesmen of the Employers that, after the war, the workers would have to be content with longer hours. Here then is the secret of the determination to crush by any and every means attempts to secure shorter hours.

The organised workers of Scotland put forward an orderly and legitimate demand for the Forty Hours. The Government's reply is bludgeons, machine-guns, bayonets and tanks. In one word, the institution of a Reign of Terror.

FELLOW-WORKERS!
Railwaymen, Miners, and all Workers of Scotland, England and Wales,
Rally to the support of your comrades on the Clyde!

Are you prepared to support us in the struggle of organised labour to obtain better conditions and to decrease unemployment? Or are you prepared to see your organisations broken and terrorised, your Council Chambers raided, your own elected spokesmen insulted, bludgeoned, and imprisoned?

Stand, then, shoulder to shoulder with us on the Clyde, and prove that organised labour is a force to be reckoned with, not something to be despised or broken.

Every man, therefore, to his Trade Union Branch—
PROTEST, AGITATE, and ORGANISE!

On behalf of the Joint Committee,

D. S. MORTON,
W. SHAW, } *Joint Secys.*
S. NIMLIN,
T. MITCHELL, *Chairman.*

SOCIALIST LABOUR PRESS Printers, 50 Renfrew Street, Glasgow.

179

43. The Railwaymen's Strike, 1919

[*A NATIONAL railway strike was called for on 26th September, 1919, because the Government was insisting on large reductions in wages as the cost of living fell. The agreement, reached on 5th October was on the whole favourable to the men.*]

THE GOVERNMENT OFFER

TO THE

Classes of Railwaymen involved in the present dispute.

THIS shows the Pre-War Wage, the Present Wage, and the Minimum Wage. The present wage is guaranteed till 31st March, 1920, after which the Government have offered to adjust it either according to the present scale, depending on the cost of living, or by Court of Arbitration, or by any other method which may be agreed between the Government and the Railwaymen.

	Pre-War Wages	Till 31st March, 1920 Present Wages Guaranteed.	Minimum wage which will not be reduced however much the cost of living falls.	After 31st March, 1920. War Bonus which continues till cost of living falls and then can only be altered by agreement or arbitration.
Porters	16s. to 22s.	49s. to 55s.	40s. to 49s.	9s. to 6s.
Parcel Porters	22s. to 30s.	53s. to 63s.	45s. to 54s.	8s. to 9s.
Ticket Collectors	21s. to 31s.	54s. to 64s.	45s. to 54s.	9s. to 10s.
Passenger Guards	25s. to 35s.	58s. to 68s.	48s. to 60s.	10s. to 8s.
Goods Guards	25s. to 35s.	58s. to 68s.	48s. to 60s.	10s. to 8s.
Shunters	20s. to 31s.	53s. to 64s.	46s. to 60s.	7s. to 4s.
Goods Porters	20s. to 26s.	53s. to 59s.	40s. to 47s.	13s. to 12s.
Checkers	21s. to 31s.	54s. to 64s.	46s. to 55s.	8s. to 9s.
Carmen	20s. to 29s.	53s. to 62s.	45s. to 52s.	8s. to 10s.
Platelayers	21s. to 24s.	54s. to 57s.	40s. to 50s.	14s. to 7s.

NOTE 1. The lower rates apply chiefly in the country; the higher rates in industrial areas.
NOTE 2. As the cost of living falls the pound is worth more and real wages increase; that is, your pound purchases more.

Why have the leaders of the Railway Unions forced a strike now?

IS THE STRIKE JUSTIFIED?

Full page Government advertisement which appeared in "The Times", 4th October, 1919

WHO IS SPEAKING THE TRUTH ?

The Government says it offers

	Government Offer Standard Wage	War Wages Bonus	Total of Government Offer
Porters - - -	40s. to 49s.	9s. to 6s.	49s. to 55s.
Parcel Porters -	45s. to 54s.	8s. to 9s.	53s. to 63s.
Ticket Collectors -	45s. to 54s.	9s. to 10s.	54s. to 64s.
Passenger Guards	48s. to 60s.	10s. to 8s.	58s. to 68s.
Goods Guards -	48s. to 60s.	10s. to 8s.	58s. to 68s.
Shunters - - -	46s. to 60s.	7s. to 4s.	53s. to 64s.
Goods Porters- -	40s. to 47s.	13s. to 12s.	53s. to 59s.
Checkers - - -	46s. to 55s.	8s. to 9s.	54s. to 64s.
Carmen - - -	45s. to 52s.	8s. to 10s.	53s to 62s.
Platelayers - - -	40s. to 50s.	14s. to 7s.	54s. to 57s.

It is not true that the figures in Column 3 are, as the Government says, its " offer."

They include the very War Bonus in Column 2 which the Government is attacking.

WORKERS IN OTHER TRADES!

Do you want **your** wages to be reduced in the same way!

Remember what the Prime Minister said: "Whatever we lay down with regard to the Railwaymen you may depend upon it is going to be claimed throughout the Country."

YOUR TURN COMES NEXT.

STAND BY THE RAILWAYMEN.

Issued by the

NATIONAL UNION OF RAILWAYMEN,

Unity House, Euston Road, N.W.1.

*Full page N.U.R. advertisement which appeared in "The Times",
4th October, 1919*

44. The General Strike, 1926

[*THE General Strike of 1926 was called by the trade unions in sympathy with the struggle of the Miners' Federation against the coal-owners. In 1925, the Government granted the owners a subsidy and at the same time set up the Samuel Commission to inquire into the state of the industry. When the Government subsidy expired in May, 1926, the owners announced they would not continue to employ the miners except at lower rates than before. In consequence the T.U.C. called a conference of its constituent unions and reported that it could see no alternative to a general sympathetic strike as a means of furthering the miners cause. The executives resolved that a strike be called as from midnight 3/4th May.*]

THE STRIKE BEGINS

"Tuesday, May 4th, started with the workers answering the call. What a wonderful response! What loyalty!! What solidarity!!! From John O'Groats to Land's End the workers answered the call to arms to defend us, to defend the brave miner in his fight for a living wage.

Hurriedly the General Council formed their Committees, made preparations to face this colossal task — the first in the history of this country.

No one could over estimate the greatness of the task that faced the General Council, and to the credit of many of the members — especially Ernest Bevin — they made every effort possible to bring into being machinery to cope with the requirements.

Unfortunately for the miners, Mr. Tom Richards, one of our representatives on the General Council, was too ill to attend; while Mr. Robert Smillie, our other representative (who, I may say, valiantly supported me on Sunday, May 2nd, before the General Council), had on Monday, May 3rd, left for Scotland, believing, I presume, that his presence was necessary among his own folk, and expecting his colleagues on the T.U.C. to continue the struggle in a straight and honourable way.

Thus the miners were left during these nine days — heroic in the fighting field and tragic in the Council — without any representation on the Council. Our President and Treasurer, and myself — the three miners' officials — were allowed to attend the meetings in the same capacity as Mr. McDonald and Mr. Henderson. I appealed to the Council to allow two of our representatives to be co-opted for the time being, but this request was refused, and was most vehemently opposed by the Rt. Hon. J. H. Thomas. We were not allowed to take part or to vote on any of the decisions.

It would not only be an education to the workers, but it would be material that could guide us in our future struggles if a verbatim report could be printed of all that took place. Unfortunately it was decided that no shorthand notes should be taken. So I am afraid the full truth will never be told.

The difficulties of transport, of communication, of giving information, was enormous; but the foresight and energy of the officials in the country and of the rank and file rose to the occasion. Links were formed, bulletins were issued; officials, staff and voluntary workers of the T.U.C. and the Labour Party worked night and day to create the machinery necessary to link up the whole movement — machinery that would have been prepared by commonsense leadership months and months before.

It was a wonderful achievement, a wonderful accomplishment that proved conclusively that the Labour Movement has the men and women that are capable in an emergency of providing the means of carrying on the country. Who can forget the effect of motor conveyances with posters saying: "By Permission of the T.U.C.?" The Government with its O.M.S. were absolutely demoralised. Confidence, calm, and order prevailed everywhere, despite the irritation caused by the volunteers, black-legs, and special constables. The workers acted as one. Splendid discipline! Splendid loyalty!

Then the question is asked: "Why was the strike called off?"...

There are, I am aware, on the General Council a number of men and women whose only object was to serve the best interests of the miners, who worked night and day to that end. But they were guided in their final decisions by the Negotiating Committee, of whom J. H. Thomas was the determining voice . . .

Enters on the scene the Chairman of the Coal Commission, Sir Herbert Samuel. He had returned post haste to England from abroad. Whether he was sent for or whether he returned voluntarily, I do not know, but the fact, nevertheless, remains that as soon as he arrived in England he was seen by the Rt. Hon. J. H. Thomas and others, and discussions began in private. Those who had been unwilling and hesitant to go into the strike were continually seeking some way out of it.

On Sunday, May 9th, it was quite evident that these discussions and pow-wows had reached a stage when the Negotiating Committee and the leaders of the Labour Party felt that something tangible had been secured to justify a move towards calling off the General Strike.

These discussions were held simply with a view to creating some pretext to justify calling off the General Strike. That is my opinion based on facts as I have seen them.

Discussions, especially with Thomas and Bromley, were such as to lead me to that conclusion; and we were again pressed by certain individuals to consider proposals for a reduction of wages. Attempts were being made by the Negotiating Committee of the T.U.C., to draft new formulae — to use the expression of our President, Herbert Smith, "To provide a new suit of clothes for the same body."

Here I must again declare my pride of our President, Herbert Smith, who, in his own Yorkshire dialect, defended the miners' case heroically. Every one of my Committee felt proud of the determined stand of our President, who did not mince his words, but spoke straight and to the point. Some of the members of the General Council will never forget Herbert Smith!

It did seem terrible that we had to fight, not only the Government and the coalowners, but certain Labour leaders as well. However, Herbert Smith was not made of the stuff that could be intimidated. The more they attacked him the stronger he became, and whatever may be the consequences or the results of our struggle, I shall ever remember the stand made by Herbert Smith, which should lead every miner to revere him to the end of his days.

Whatever Herbert Smith may not be able to do, nobody can charge him with not being able to fight clean and straight for the men that he has so ably represented.

May 9th, 10th and 11th were days of numerous meetings. There were long discussions in the T.U.C. There were also numerous meetings between the T.U.C. Negotiating Committee and Sir Herbert Samuel.

On Monday evening the 10th, proposals were drafted, accepted by the Negotiating Committee, and placed before the full Executive of the Miners' Federation. They were amended and sent back to the T.U.C., but rejected by them.

Tuesday, 11th, again several meetings. All these in our absence. Only once were we called over to see Sir Herbert Samuel, on Monday, 10th, when our President, myself and Mr. Richardson made our position quite clear. Nevertheless the T.U.C. Negotiating Committee continued in their feverish desire to lift the General Strike without securing protection for the miners. And, as has since been learnt, without even securing protection for their own members against victimisation.

On Tuesday morning the Miners' Executive met and reviewed the position in various Districts. With the knowledge that these negotiations were going on behind our backs, the Executive determined nevertheless that it would stand fast by its colours.

It is characteristic of the difficulties we were contending with, that, although I issued to the Press a statement embodying our viewpoint (I was obliged to do this to contradict a lying story circulated by a Press Agency) in the afternoon and even the scab capitalist press all printed it, no mention appeared in the workers' own official, the *British Worker*.

At 8 o'clock on Tuesday evening the whole of my colleagues – the full Committee – were called before the General Council and informed by the chairman that a unanimous decision had been arrived at. Proposals had been received from Sir Herbert Samuel and agreed upon by the Negotiating Committee of the General Council.

In a long speech, Mr. Pugh solemnly and seriously declared that the General Council had decided that these proposals must be accepted by the miners' representatives as a basis for negotiations, and that they would call off the strike. They had guarantees that satisfied them that the Government would accept these proposals, and that on the strike being withdrawn the lock-out notices also would be withdrawn, and the miners should return to work on the status quo (with, of course, a reduction in wages to come after resumption of work). We were told these proposals were unalterable, could not be amended, that we had to accept them en bloc as this was the unanimous decision of the T.U.C.

Mr. Pugh was continually pressed and questioned by Mr. Herbert Smith, myself, and my colleagues as to what the guarantees mentioned were, and who had given them. We got no answer. But J. H. Thomas said to me personally, when I asked him whether the Government would accept the Samuel proposals and what were his guarantees: "You may not trust my word, but will you not accept the word of a British gentleman who has been Governor of Palestine?"

Our President, myself and my colleagues put several other questions; asking what was the position of other workers in regard to the unanimous decision arrived at that we should all return to work together, to protect one another from victimisation, and to secure a return by all workers on the same conditions as when they left. We were informed that "That was all right." We continually pressed this point, when J. H. Thomas replied: "I have seen to it that the members of the railways will be protected" –

187

the inference being that we need not trouble to meddle with the business of other unions.

I will allow the railwaymen to now judge whether the "protection" given them had any real existence.

Herbert Smith made our position quite clear, and again courageously faced the General Council, knowing well what the consequences might be.

What was the situation with which we were confronted? Before myself and my colleagues an abyss had opened. It was the culmination of days and days of faint heartedness. It had begun even before the General Strike with the attempt to use this magnificent expression of working-class solidarity as a mere bluff — albeit, gigantic bluff.

To prevent that bluff being called they had been prepared (on Saturday and Sunday and Monday, from the 1st to 3rd of May) to give away all the T.U.C. had stood for. They had been prepared to force *us* to retreat in order that *they* might carry out the retreat they longed for. When the truculence of the Tory Cabinet thrust them willy nilly into the General Strike they had not ceased in their endeavour to "smooth it over."

Only a few days of magnificent working class effort had passed before they were once more trying to get a peace at any price. Then, gradually, an incredible thing happened. They began to win over one after another of their colleagues on the G.C. Bit by bit the process of "persuading" the others went on until the situation of complete surrender had been reached, the situation with which we now faced. It was more than a surrender on their part. It was an ultimatum to us as miners, bidding us surrender, too!

We decided to adjourn as a committee to a room in the Labour Party offices next door, to consider the position, and the following resolution was arrived at:—

"The Miners' Executive have given careful and patient consideration to the draft proposals prepared by the T.U.C. Negotiating Committee and endorsed by the General Council as

188

representing 'the best terms which can be obtained to settle the present crisis in the Coal Industry.

They regret the fact that no opportunity for consideration was afforded the accredited representatives of the Miners' Federation on the Negotiating Committee in the preparation of the draft or in the discussion of May 11th leading thereto.

"At best, the proposals imply a reduction of the wages rates of a large number of mineworkers, which is contrary to the repeated declarations of the Miners' Federation, and which they believe their fellow Trade Unionists are assisting them to resist.

"They regret therefore, whilst having regard to the grave issues involved, that they must reject the proposals. Moreover, if such proposals are submitted as a means to call off the General Strike such a step must be taken on the sole responsibility of the General Council."

This resolution was taken to the General Council just after midnight on Tuesday, 11th. We had not then been informed that arrangements had been made to meet the Prime Minister that night, and that a telephone communication had been sent through from Downing Street, asking Mr. Citrine "when the Negotiating Committee would be done." That I learnt from other quarters, but is nevertheless a fact which cannot be denied.

But owing to the attitude of the miners, who refused to swallow the decision of the General Council – believing that there were not sufficient guarantees to secure the protection of our men, and also with the knowledge that the Samuel proposals meant reductions in wages for our men – no meeting with the Prime Minister took place that evening.

In the early hours of Wednesday morning, after passing our resolution, we left them. We were tired and weary, almost disheartened and dejected, but firm in our conviction that we had done the right thing and remained loyal and honourable to the trust placed in our hands by the million miners and their dependents; and also believing that the whole rank and file of our movement were out in defence of the miners' standard of living.

Nothing has taken place since to change that attitude.

Wednesday, May 12th, at 10 a.m., the Miners' Committee met — we had informed the General Council of that. Another episode I shall never forget. When leaving the Council Chamber, Ramsay MacDonald approached me and asked if he could come to see us and help us in this business as this "was a tragic blunder." I replied: "No, you have already taken your stand in appealing to us to consider reductions and the full acceptance of the Samuel Report, which meant reductions. That has been your attitude throughout, and we do not want you to come to our meeting."

At the hotel where I was staying, the National Hotel, I received a message on Wednesday morning saying that the officials were required at Eccleston Square. My colleagues and myself did not go, but attended our Executive, and I was later informed that a deputation was attending from the General Council. The following members of the General Council came, Pugh, Purcell, Walker, Bevin, Ben Turner, and Rowan, with two others.

They placed before my Committee the decision that had been arrived at by the General Council after we had left them. The decision was that they had arranged to meet the Prime Minister at 12 o'clock that day to call off the General Strike on the basis of the Samuel Proposals, as they believed there were sufficient guarantees, etc. They appealed to the miners to throw in their lot with them and join them in that decision.

After several questions and discussions — again concerning securities and guarantees, etc., the Miners' Executive arrived at the following conclusion:—

"That having heard the report of the representatives of the T.U.C., we reaffirm our resolution of May 11th, and express our profound admiration to the wonderful demonstration of loyalty as displayed by all workers who promptly withdrew their labour in support of the miners' standards, and undertake to report fully to a Conference to be convened as early as practicable."

I informed Mr. Bevin and the representatives of this, and they left the office at 11-45 a.m. for Downing Street.

This is all we know of the tragic decision, arrived at in our absence, to call off the General Strike. The verbatim report of the interview with the Prime Minister speaks for itself. No statement seemed to have been made by anyone except Bevin regarding the raising of the lock-out and the protection of our men. It seemed that the only desire of some leaders was to call off the General Strike at any cost, without any guarantees for the workers, miners, or others.

By this action of theirs, in "turning off the power," the miners were left alone in their struggle.

A few days longer and the Government and the capitalist class, financiers, parasites and exploiters, would have been compelled to make peace with the miners. We should thus have secured in the mining industry a settlement which would have redounded to the honour and credit of the British Labour Movement, and would have been a fitting reward for the solidarity displayed by the workers.

They threw away the chance of a victory greater than any British Labour has ever won.

That is the history of the Nine Days which gave an unexampled display of the solidarity of the workers. It is quite evident that some of the T.U.C. were afraid of the power they had created; were anxious to keep friends with the Government and not to harm the employing class. They did not understand the task – at least a great many of them did not – and there were others who were determined to sabotage the General Strike to justify their repeated declarations, "that it would not succeed."

First they declared the rank and file would not respond to a sympathetic strike. Then after the rank and file had responded they continued to try and prove that it would not succeed.

They are still trying to prove it, but while some leaders have declared "Never again," and others have tried to say – as the leader of the Labour Party did in "Answers" – that the strike is a useless weapon, those of us who saw the shattering effect it had on British capitalism and the strike forward in solidarity made by our own people realise that the General Strike did not fail.

191

Since May 12th we have been left to continue our struggle alone — but not alone, as the rank and file are still with us. They did not let us down. Our bus-men, car-men, rail-men, and dock-men, men from the desks — pens laid aside — printers and press-men, engineers and electricity men from the rank and file. All joined together with one motto: "Solidarity for Ever — and Capitalism defied!"

As miners we thank them. For us they refused to bend; for us they struck our rights to defend. With such support our cause will not fail, for we all believe right will in the end prevail.

So ended the Nine Days of Labour's united struggle. We still continue, believing that the whole rank and file will help us all they can. We appeal for financial help wherever possible, and that our comrades will still refuse to handle coal so that we may yet secure victory for the miners' wives and children who will live to thank the rank and file of the Unions of Great Britain. We hope still that those leaders of the T.U.C. who feel that a mistake has been made will rally to our cause and help us·to victory."

A. J. COOK, *The Nine Days — The Story of the General Strike told by the Miners' Secretary* (1926)

45. The Strikers' Alphabet, 1926

[*WITH the absence of newspapers during the General Strike, many local strike committees issued their own duplicated bulletins. Often these contained notes or verses on the strike written by strikers, and popular features were copied by other bulletins. The following was printed in the St. Pancras (London) Bulletin in instalments in Nos. 2-9, 5th-10th May, 1926.*]

"A is for ALL, ALL OUT and ALL WIN,
And down with the blacklegs and scabs who stay in.
B is for Baldwin, the Bosses' Strong Man,
But he's welcome to dig all the coal that he can.
C is for Courage the workers have shown,
Class Conscious and Confident that they'll hold their own.
D is for DOPE that the Government spread —
Dishwash for Duncos and Dubbs — "nuf sed."
E is for Energy that will carry us through,
Everyone class-conscious, steadfast and true.
F is for fight, our fight to the end,
For we're solid together, not an inch will we bend.
G is for Grab-all, the bosses, you know,
Greedy and grasping, one day they must go.
H is Hardship, we all must endure;
However, keep smiling, for Victory is sure.
I is for Interest, Profits and Rent
Into the pockets of the Indolent.
J is for Jix, the stirrer of strife,
Just waiting the chance to have your life.
K is for knife that is wielded by Jix,
Keep yourselves orderly and frustrate his tricks.
L is for London, where the T.U.C. meet,
Leading the workers the bosses to beat.

M is for Miners, for whose rights we must fight,
Maintaining the cause which we know to be right.
N is for Natsopa, who stopped dope from the Boss,
Narking Churchill and Jix, so Baldwin was cross.
O is for O.M.S., the scabbing patrol;
Oh! how they are working, digging the Coal!!
P is for pickets on guard at the gates,
Pulling up blacklegs who scab on their mates.
Q is for Quandary the Government's in,
Quite certain now the workers will win.
R is for Railways that won't run alone,
Ready for workers to run as their own.
S is for Solidarity that is winning our fight;
Stick well together, for Victory's in sight.
T is for Taximen joined in the fray,
Troubling the blacklegs to walk all the way.
U is for Unity, each one for all,
United we stand till the Government fall.
V is for Victory, of which we are sure,
Vanquishing the bosses for evermore.
W is for Workers' Wages and hours,
We are nearing the day when control is ours.
X is for eXit the whole boss class –
Xtra enjoyment for me and my lass.
Y is for Young Workers to whom fighting is new;
Yes, Young, but determined to fight with you.
Z is for Zeal shown by the Vigilance Corps,
Zealous that workers aren't trapped by the law."

Appendix: A Striker's Handbook

[*CONSIDERING the number of strikes which take place and the numbers of people involved in them, it is surprising how little printed and available guidance there is for so widespread a human activity. An exception is the remarkable document adopted by the Red International of Labour Unions (a Communist international union body now defunct) in 1929 at their Strassburg meeting, and published in Britain by the National Minority Movement in 1932.*]

"STRIKE STRATEGY AND TACTICS
(The Lessons of the Industrial Struggles)

I. PREPARATION OF THE MASSES FOR STRIKES
AND LOCK-OUTS

The experience of recent strikes in France, Germany and Poland shows that they were inadequately prepared. If the workers are not to be taken unawares the trade union opposition and the independent revolutionary unions must carry on their work as follows:

1. The daily work of the revolutionary unions and the trade union opposition in every branch of industry must consist in preparing the workers for coming conflicts between Labour and Capital.

2. At the first sign of discontent among the workers, or aggressive intentions on the part of the employers against the workers, the workers of the respective industry must be warned of the fact that a collision is imminent.

3. The agitational and organization preliminary work should be carried on under the following slogans: "Do not expect anything of the reformist leaders; they will betray you"; "Be masters of your own destiny"; "Prepare for the struggle, otherwise you

195

will be defeated." In this agitation full use should be made of concrete cases of treachery on the part of the trade union bureaucrats in the recent industrial struggles.

4. Already during this preparatory period it will be necessary to find out at meetings and by personal intercourse which are the elements in the circles of non-Party, anarcho-syndicalist, reformist or Christian workers who can be drawn into the struggle against the employers on the basis of our tactics of complete independence from the trade union bureaucrats, and who can also participate, together with the revolutionary workers, in the organs created for the preparation and leadership of the struggle.

5. The economic demands must be clear and accessible to the masses; they should have their origin in the respective concrete situation and should be discussed with the workers interested in them, in order that they should be a means of winning over the majority of the workers and serve as a basis for a united front from below and for united action.

6. In the preparatory period conferences of representatives of enterprises or of factory councils can play an important rôle, provided the latter are not under the influence of the reformists and not organs of class collaboration.

7. The revolutionary unions and the trade union opposition must watch carefully the work of all their organs in regard to their connection with the mass of the workers in the factories, and must energetically fight any sign of red tape and dissociation from the masses, which hinders them from being able to react immediately to any development in the factories.

8. The revolutionary unions and the trade union opposition must conduct all the preparatory work in such a way that the necessity of the creation of fighting organs for the conduct of the struggle should be suggested from below by the rank and file, and should become the subject of discussion in all enterprises.

9. If a lock-out is in sight the slogan of COMMITTEES OF ACTION TO RESIST THE LOCK-OUT and of insisting on the demands of the workers is to be issued. These committees of action should be elected by all the workers of the enterprise REGARDLESS OF

PARTY and trade union membership, and regardless of being organized or not.

10. If the situation is favourable for a strike and the mass of the workers is imbued with a fighting spirit, the formation of STRIKE COMMITTEES elected by all the workers should be advocated (even if the strike is under the leadership of a revolutionary trade union). The workers of all tendencies, the organized and unorganized alike, should participate in the election of these committees.

11. Simultaneously an energetic agitation and propaganda should be carried on amongst the masses against the APPOINTMENT OF STRIKE COMMITTEES FROM ABOVE, and against the attempts of the trade union bureaucrats to entrust such committees with leadership of the conflicts.

12. The preparation of the industrial masses for the struggle must be by word of mouth and through the Press. In this respect the trade union and Party press must take upon itself a very serious task. Very desirable is the publication of leaflets, special supplements to the press organs, factory newspapers, etc., dealing especially with the expected conflict.

13. The most dangerous things in industrial struggles are experimental calls and invitations to strike based on sentiment instead of common sense. Not only thorough knowledge of the respective branch of industry is expected of the leaders, but also thorough information as to what is going on among the masses. The main thing is not to intervene too late, not to lag behind the masses, to take advantage of their will to fight, and at the same time not to declare a strike without having prepared the masses thoroughly for it.

14. Of special importance is the selection of the right moment for the declaration of the strike. In this respect the Lodz experiences (as regards the selection of the right moment) must be, of course, taken into consideration. If the right moment is missed this will certainly lead to an unfavourable result of the conflict. Therefore the outbreak of the strike must be fixed at a moment favourable to the workers as regards the industrial and political

situation, time and place, correlation of forces, employers' policy, etc.

15. In the preparatory period the question of strike and lock-out funds must be seriously considered, especially in countries and trade unions where strike funds do not exist. If it is wrong to expect that the workers can beat the employers with the help of their trade union funds, it is also wrong to think of help for strikers and locked-out workers when the struggle has already begun (France).

II. FORMS, NATURE AND FUNCTIONS OF THE
FIGHTING ORGANS

The object of the whole preparatory work is — to explain to the interested masses the necessity of a properly organized struggle. This is so important that we must popularize among the masses the idea of anti-lock-out committees, strike committees and special commissions for the conduct of the struggle. Whenever a lock-out is expected committees should be elected to struggle against it, and the election of strike committees should be taken in hand several days before the declaration of the strike.

The election of the strike or anti-lock-out committee is to take place several days before the lock-out sets in or the strike is declared. If the lock-out sets in suddenly, or if the strike breaks out unexpectedly and the election of proper committees cannot take place at the right time, a factory meeting (embracing all departments) should be called as soon as the strike or lock-out begins, before the workers have left the enterprise. At this meeting, after the necessary preliminary remarks, the election of a committee should be proposed and a list of candidates (prepared beforehand) from the midst of revolutionary, anarcho-syndicalist, reformist, Christian and non-Party workers should be brought forward.

To ensure a satisfactory COMPOSITION of the strike committees they should be elected in the factories, and even in the bigger departments of the latter, in order to arrive at a proper representation of all categories and groups of workers – as, for instance, THE SHOP DELEGATIONS IN LODZ.

The mode of election should be determined by the extent of the conflict and the size of the enterprise. The bigger the strike committee is, the easier it will be for it to lead the mass of the strikers. In smaller enterprises there should be to every twenty-five to fifty workers one member on the strike committee; in bigger enterprises one member to every 100 to 200 workers. In big enterprises employing tens of thousands of workers the strike committees must consist of 200 to 300 members, so that they shall be directly connected with all the departments of the enterprise through the elected members. Such large strike committees must elect an executive, whose business it will be to call the members of the committee together regularly, to report to them, to inform them and to keep in contact with the strikers through them, a definite duty being assigned for this purpose to every member of the strike committee. As to the functions and tasks of the strike committee, efforts should be made in the following direction:

1. It is incumbent on the strike committee to carry on with all the means at its disposal the struggle for the realization of the workers' demands. The success of the struggle will depend on the measure of the strike committee's success in eliminating the influence of the reformist trade union apparatus and wrestling from it the leadership of the strike.

2. The strike committee must lead the struggle, enter into negotiations, eventually sign agreements, declaring beforehand that all arrangements made by the reformist bureaucrats behind the back of the strikers cannot be binding on the workers.

3. The strike committee must carefully watch the activity of the trade union bureaucrats; in case of negotiations and machinations behind the scenes, it must organize demonstrations outside the trade union premises, call meetings of organized and unorganized workers, demand the resignation of reactionary trade union bureaucrats, collect money and help all the strikers, as well as systematically undermine the confidence of the workers, especially

the Social-Democratic and Christian workers, in the reformist or Christian trade union apparatus.

4. The strike committee must become a powerful weapon in the hands of the trade union opposition for the purpose of removing from the unions all the agents of the capitalists and the allies of the employers.

5. The strike committee must draw the factory councils into the struggle. But if they choose to side with the trade union bureaucrats ruthless struggle should be carried on against them as well as against the trade union bureaucrats.

6. The main task of the strike committee does not only consist in drawing the attention of the masses to the slogans brought forward in our struggle, but also — AND THIS IS PARTICULARLY IMPORTANT — in supplementing and extending the original slogans, and in issuing new political slogans in accordance with any new situation or change of circumstances, without ever letting initiative slip from its hands.

7. A strike committee must on no account adopt the standpoint "all or nothing." In the course of the campaign the strike committee must be able to estimate correctly the correlation of forces and to manoeuvre (of course not in the sense of arrangements on top). We have learned by experience that lack of elasticity is a great mistake in the revolutionary class struggle.

8. If a strike or lock-out is to be given a proper lead the lock-out or strike committees must represent the whole of the workers involved in the conflict. In the event of bigger lock-outs or strikes involving a whole series of enterprises in a big district, or a whole branch of industry, a central strike committee must be formed which will represent the local strike committees.

9. The democratically elected strike or lock-out committee must establish strict discipline to ensure the success of the struggle.

10. When anti-lock-out and strike committees or other fighting organs are elected for the forthcoming struggle, provision must be made for the right to recall members of these organs who are not doing their duty in regard to the energetic conduct of the struggle, and are thereby going against the wish of their electors.

11. Anti-lock-out and strike committees and other fighting organs have not only to see to a regular registration of all workers involved in the conflict; they must also promote the establishment of control bureaus, in order to strengthen connections and draw as many workers as possible into active participation in the struggle.

12. The strike committees must keep up a close connection between the strikers and the unemployed in order to prevent unemployed workers being used for the breaking up of the industrial struggle.

III. OUR TACTICS IN THE DEMOCRATICALLY ELECTED STRIKE COMMITTEES

The strike committee, as an organ elected by the mass of the workers, consists necessarily of workers of various tendencies, and in the initial stage of the struggle the adherents of the R.I.L.U. are likely to be in a minority. In such cases the revolutionary workers must display the utmost circumspection, tact and understanding in order to win the majority for the revolutionary tactics. Above all, the adherents of the R.I.L.U. must be the best disciplined and most unselfish members of the strike committee whenever it is a question of accentuating and extending the struggle. At all the sessions of the strike committee they must criticise indecision and wobbling, and must expose the machinations of the reformist and Christian spokesmen. If wobbling is noticeable in the strike committee the adherents of the R.I.L.U. must demand that the question of the continuation of the struggle be brought up for decision at mass meetings of the workers. If this demand be rejected the election of a new strike committee, of more determined and persevering leaders, must be proposed to the masses. If the revolutionary minority resigns from the strike committee which has come under the influence of the reformists, the minority must appeal to the masses and organize the election of a new strike committee for the continuation of the struggle. In very extreme cases the revolutionary wing can and must resign from the strike

201

committee if the majority gets under the influence of the reformists and throttles the strike, while the mass of the workers are determined to continue the struggle. The adherents of the R.I.L.U. must establish control of the masses over the activity and conduct of the strike committee, and must struggle energetically against the strike committee being degraded into an auxiliary organ of the union, as happened in North France, even in the case of a revolutionary union. The most important task of the adherents of the R.I.L.U. in regard to strike committees is the election – by democratic methods – of their best and most energetic functionaries to these organs, who must secure a leading position within them through their energetic and exemplary work carried out in the class spirit, must always act in an organized manner in these committees without ever becoming dissociated from the masses who have elected them, and must carry with them the workers of all tendencies, resting always on the confidence of the masses. It is incumbent on the adherents of the R.I.L.U. to strengthen the confidence of the masses in these fighting organs, and actually to lead them through the non-party strike and anti-lock-out committees.

IV. TO LEAD AND NOT TO COMMAND!

A strike or lock-out which sets big sections of workers in motion creates a favourable situation for an extension of the revolutionary wing of the Labour movement. But this influence can only be extended if the leading elements get into contact with the masses and secure healthy relations between the strike committee and the strikers. The strike committee must be able to keep continually in contact with the masses; it must realize the importance of regular reporting and must be always ready to strengthen its composition by co-opting new energetic members; it must carry on its work so that it can be controlled by every worker. It is very dangerous for the strike committee to assume a hectoring tone in regard to the strikers when trying to settle im-

portant questions off its own bat, or going even the length of renouncing certain demands or putting an end to the strike. The
system of commands and secret diplomacy must be eliminated
from the practice of strike committees, whose rôle and importance
cannot grow unless they be under the control of the masses and
decide in conjunction with them all important strike questions.
Control over the activities of the strike committees by the strikers
and contact between this committee and the masses does not, of
course, mean that the strike committee is not to make independent
decisions when they do not brook delay, accounting for them subsequently to the masses. In this respect the lessons of the recent
strikes must be carefully studied, and whenever a strike committee
assumes a hectoring tone it must be severely criticized.

V. RELATIONS BETWEEN THE STRIKE COMMITTEES AND REFORMIST TRADE UNION APPARATUS

The reformists are either appointing strike committees themselves or are insisting on participation in them. The Lodz experience has shown that the admission of representatives of reformist
unions to the strike committees means the beginning of the defeat.
Therefore everything should be done to protect strike committees
from being influenced by the Social-Democrats and the reformist
trade union bureaucrats; there must be energetic opposition to
the co-option of official representatives of the reformist unions
to the strike committees. OFFICIAL REPRESENTATIVES OF THE
REFORMIST UNIONS SHOULD ON NO ACCOUNT BE ADMITTED TO
STRIKE COMMITTEES. All the attempts of the reformists to penetrate into the strike committees must be met by the adherents of
the R.I.L.U. with the demand that all members of the strike committee must be elected by all the organized and unorganized
workers. Energetic opposition must also be offered to the reformists' attempts to have the strike committees elected only by
trade union members. IF THE STRIKE BE FORMALLY LED BY A
REFORMIST UNION ONE OR TWO REPRESENTATIVES OF THIS

UNION WITH A CONSULTATIVE VOTE CAN BE ADMITTED IN ORDER THAT THEY COULD REPORT ON THE DOINGS OF THE COMMITTEE OF THEIR UNION. All attempts to relax during a strike the struggle against the trade union bureaucrats under the pretext that they are at the head of the strike must be energetically opposed. It is just during the strike movement that one must make tenfold efforts to expose the reformist trade union bureaucrats, their strike-breaking methods and prevarications, their flirtation with the bourgeoisie and the bourgeois State, etc. This exposure is to take place not only through the Party press and the press of the trade union opposition, but especially through the strike committee, because it is only by setting the strike committee against the ruling reformist trade union apparatus that a truly independent leadership of industrial struggles can be enforced. THE LEAST IDEOLOGICAL AND ORGANISATIONAL DEPENDENCE OF THE STRIKE COMMITTEE ON THE REFORMIST TRADE UNION APPARATUS, THE LEAST RELAXATION OF THE STRUGGLE AGAINST THE LATTER, CAN LEAD TO THE DEFEAT OF THE STRIKE AND CAN IMPAIR THE AUTHORITY OF THE TRADE UNION OPPOSITION AND THAT OF THE STRIKE COMMITTEES WHICH WERE FORMED AT ITS INITIATIVE.

VI. THE UNITED-FRONT PROBLEM DURING STRIKES AND LOCK-OUTS

The usual excitement of the masses when a conflict is expected is favourable to the creation of the united front from below. Before the outbreak of the conflict it is necessary to proceed from agitation and propaganda for the united front to organizational steps. In this direction the following is necessary:

1. Election of the best and most experienced workers of all tendencies — Communists, Social-Democratic, Christian, unorganized, etc. — to all elective organs.

2. Strike committees must entrust workers of various political groupings with reporting on the work done in order thereby to do

away with the reporting monopoly of the Christians and Social-Democrats among the Christian and Social-Democratic trade unions.

3. Non-party and reformist workers should be entrusted with all kinds of functions in order to draw them into direct collaboration and participation in the struggle.

4. When non-party, Christian and Social-Democratic workers report on the activity of the strike committees they must see that these reports are published in their press.

5. Very useful in time of strikes or lock-outs is the organization of special conferences of organized and unorganized men and women workers, adult and adolescent, in order to promote the best and most active among them to posts of militant leadership.

6. Special attention should be paid in time of strikes and lock-outs that all arrangements between leaders and the formation of a united front from above be energetically opposed.

7. Adherents of the R.I.L.U. who make agreements with the reformist leaders *re* mutual forbearance during the strike, and renounce mutual criticism, etc., must be relentlessly condemned. This is not a united front, but a very bad caricature of it.

8. The object of the united front during a strike or lock-out is to raise the fighting capacity of the masses, and not the mutual insurance of the leaders. Therefore we must aim at a close union with the workers in the reformist organizations and must carry on at the same time a ruthless struggle against the reformist trade union bureaucrats.

9. One of the most effective united-front methods by which one can weld together the ranks of the struggling workers is the organization of mass demonstrations and processions under the leadership of elected fighting organs against the bourgeois and Social-Democratic police and municipal authorities.

10. The united front from below, skilfully applied during the struggle, must be fully utilized at the end of the struggle for the establishment of closer contact between the masses and the adherents of the R.I.L.U. The forms in which this should be done must be adapted to the respective country and the branch of

industry, to the correlation of forces in the working class, etc. The results must be certainly utilized and consolidated.

VII. STRIKE PICKETS AND SELF-DEFENCE CORPS

The success of the strike depends in many cases on the mode of the organization of the strike pickets, and on the ability of the strikers to frustrate the devices of the corrupt employers' gangs of blacklegs. In this connection the organization of strike pickets and self-defence corps assumes considerable importance. The strike committees have to act as follows in this sphere:

1. The strike pickets should, of course, consist of workers of all tendencies, and the self-defence corps must be organized in a manner to allow the co-operation of experienced comrades with unorganized, Social-Democratic and Christian workers.

2. The strike pickets must be carefully selected; they must not only consist of young workers, but also of older working men and women, and especially of working men's wives.

3. The widest possible working-class circles should be drawn into mass picketing in order to keep as many workers as possible occupied.

4. It is very useful to organise special demonstrations of working men's wives and children against blacklegs and the police forces called out to protect them.

5. Picket duty is the DUTY of all strikers; not a single worker must be allowed to get out of doing something during the conflict.

6. In Fascist and White terror countries (Italy, Poland, Rumania, Bulgaria), or in countries where the employers and reformists organize strike-breaking, self-defence corps must be formed as soon as the strike breaks out, and the most active workers must be drawn into them.

7. For picketing and the self-defence corps it is desirable to use members of sport organizations and proletarian women's leagues, which can play a very important rôle during strikes.

8. The collisions between the pickets and the State authorities can serve as an illustration, not only to the pickets themselves, but

also to the mass of the strikers, of the elementary proof that coalition exists between the employers and the bourgeois State.

9. Special attention should be paid to the struggle against the various police and private detective organizations (factory police, factory spies, fire brigade as a component part of the factory police, etc.).

VIII. UNOFFICIAL STRIKES

The policy of international reformism, which aims at a "peaceable" settlement of all industrial struggles through compulsory arbitration, systematic sabotage and throttling of the demands of the workers through the reformist trade union apparatus, brings the mass of the workers face to face with the problem of struggle for the most elementary demands without or against the sanction of the reformist trade union bureaucrats. The so-called unofficial strikes, that is, strikes which are declared by the workers without the sanction and against the will of the official central organs of the respective union, strikes which were formerly resorted to every now and then, constitute now the only way of counteracting the increasing exploitation and pressure of the employers. Strikes without the sanction and against the will of the union are becoming more and more frequent. They have already become a mass phenomenon, and will continue to do so to a still greater extent.

This makes it necessary to recognize the so-called wild or unofficial strikes, whereas the trade union bureaucrats are aiming at giving up strikes altogether. Strikes which take place without or against the sanction of the reformist union, especially in countries where the trade union bureaucrats are still very strong (Germany, Great Britain), require thorough preparation on the part of the adherents of the R.I.L.U., who must strain every nerve to make them a success. We must above all overcome in our own ranks underestimation of the forces of the workers, over-estimation of the forces of the reformist trade union apparatus and fear of the trade union bureaucrats. From day to day we must carry on agitation and propaganda among the masses, pointing out that the workers have nothing to expect from the reformist trade union apparatus, as it is only an obstacle to the struggle of the workers for their most elementary demands. Whenever an unofficial strike breaks out we must rouse the initiative and energy of the masses, because it is only by urging them to participate energetically in the struggle that we can hope to make a breach in the united front of the employers, the bourgeois State and the reformist bureaucrats.

IX. THE EXTENSION OF THE FIGHTING AREA — THE PROBLEM OF RESERVES

In the present situation — trustification and concentration of capital — the working class comes face to face with the problem of reserves in every industrial conflict. As the organizations of the employers, which have inexhaustible sources of revenue at their disposal and are supported by the bourgeois State and the reformist organizations, are very powerful, every big industrial conflict assumes political importance for the whole working class. This makes the problem of EXTENDING THE STRUGGLE, attracting new sections of workers, and calling up reserves, of special importance in regard to the trend and issue of the struggle.

The extension of the struggle can be effected vertically and horizontally, *i.e.*, by getting hold of all the workers or of a considerable section of workers employed in a given industry or branch of industry, or of the workers of whole districts. In both cases the extension of the struggle IS POSSIBLE AFTER SERIOUS PRELIMINARY AND ENERGETIC AGITATION AMONG THESE CATEGORIES OF WORKERS BEFORE THE OUTBREAK OF THE STRUGGLE, AND ESPECIALLY WHILE IT IS GOING ON. The question which category of workers is to be called upon to help depends on where the employers affected by the conflict are most vulnerable. First consideration must be given to the enterprises connected with and subordinate to the respective trust; then we must turn our attention to the enterprises which supply the raw materials or manufacture the finished article. We must be prepared that the employers will in such a case place their orders somewhere else and will procure articles of which there is a shortage from other districts or from abroad, etc. A very effective weapon is to secure the assistance of the land and sea transport service, and also that of the enterprises of common utility, such as electric power stations, gas works, etc.

In all these cases the general situation must be taken into consideration; we must not only wish to extend the struggle, but must aim at extending our influence, increasing the preparedness of the masses as well as their willingness to join the struggle for the sake of solidarity. Therefore we must remember, during the preparations for and in the course of the struggle, that to isolate the movement from the wide proletarian masses of the other branches of industry would be very dangerous.

X. CONTINUATION OF STRUGGLE AFTER THE REFORMISTS HAVE THROTTLED THE STRIKE

The experience of the recent strikes in North France, the Ruhr District, Lodz, etc., has shown that, if the reformists do not manage to throttle the movement at the start, they select in the course of the struggle the suitable moment for breaking the strike in order to attack the struggling workers from the back. The reformists make use of their influence on certain sections of workers, knowing that the most passive elements are always ready to follow those who propose the cessation of the struggle, especially if this is done under the Socialist banner, and throttle systematically one mass movement after the other. Moreover, the movement is as a rule throttled by negotiations behind the scenes without the knowledge and desire of the workers. Therefore the adherents of the R.I.L.U. must demand energetically before and during the conflict that decision *re* cessation of the struggle should rest with the workers' public meetings. In all the recent strikes the strike-breaking tactics of the reformists resulted in the majority of the workers resuming work, and the question if one could and should continue the struggle in the enterprises and districts where the adherents of the R.I.L.U. have a decisive influence loomed big before the latter.

The continuation of the struggle in the Widsew and Halluin enterprises after the throttling of the general movement in Lodz and North France was perfectly correct politically and tactically.

Under such circumstances struggle is, of course, very difficult, because the strength of the workers is already broken and the retreat effected by the strike-breaking tactic of the Social-Democrats and Amsterdamers has a demoralizing effect on the strikers. Nevertheless, the continuation of the struggle is in certain cases absolutely necessary; otherwise all future strikes would be throttled owing to the systematic strike-breaking policy of the reformists. Continuation of the struggle when the majority of workers have already abandoned it demands enormous persever-ance, extraordinary unity, determination to pursue one's aim and colossal energy on the part of all workers, without exception, who have remained at their posts, for this is the only way of not only holding out but even winning such a partial struggle. One must not draw from the fact that several such strikes (the strike in the Widsew enterprise, etc.) were defeated the conclusion that this method of struggle is erroneous. The conclusion to be drawn must be that the adherents of the R.I.L.U. must multiply their efforts in such cases in order to organize and mobilize the masses through-out the country, to ensure help for the workers who are struggling in one sector of the social front.

XI. HOW CAN THE THROTTLING OF THE STRUGGLE BE PREVENTED?

The systematic strike-breaking tactics of the reformist trade union apparatus raises the question how the complete throttling of the struggle can be prevented. In this connection specific tasks which will take a long time to solve are confronting the adherents of the R.I.L.U. The mass of the workers cannot be fully protected from the throttling of the movement unless the reformist influence on the masses is completely eliminated. The more accentuated the class struggle, the more ruthless must be our struggle against the reformist agents of the capitalists among the workers. It will take many years' strenuous organizational-political and agitational-propagandist work to weld together the masses on the basis of class struggle. The date depends in this respect, on our own ability, energy, consistency and persistence on maximum perseverance and elasticity, and — what is most important — on the *tempo* of the extension of our political influence and the systematic organizational consolidation of this influence. A guide in the carrying out of these tasks is provided by the lines carefully elaborated and laid down by the congresses of the Comintern and the R.I.L.U.

The special tasks which confront the adherents of the R.I.L.U. under the present concrete circumstances, when industrial struggles are on the increase, are a different matter. In this connection a series of concrete tasks arise, the systematic carrying out of which is the premise for a successful conclusion of the respective struggle in the respective sector of the front.

If the struggle is to be successful the following is necessary:

1. The struggle against all the allies of capitalism must be accentuated, the workers being warned before the outbreak of, and particularly during the conflict, THAT THE ENEMY IS IN THEIR OWN RANKS.

2. In connection with the election of lock-out and strike committees or other fighting organs, one must refuse to have anything to do with people connected with Social-Democracy and trade union bureaucracy, as likely strike-breakers.

3. One must therefore endeavour to elect to all fighting organs people WHO HAVE PROVED by deeds, and not words, that they are championing the cause of the working class.

4. During the conflict the struggle against compulsory arbitration and other bourgeois-reformist methods of throttling the struggle must be increased tenfold.

5. The confidence of the workers in the reformist trade union apparatus and its class collaboration tactic must be undermined.

6. In the course of the strike one must react to any suspicious step of the reformist trade union leaders, not only in the press, but mainly at strike meetings, by carrying resolutions which condemn capitulation, bargaining behind the scenes and strike-breaking methods.

7. An energetic struggle must be carried on against the trade union organs (central committee, delegate meeting, etc.) making arbitrary final decisions on the cessation of the struggle. These questions must be decided by all the workers, organized and unorganized alike, and by the fighting organs elected by the mass of the workers. One should bear in mind that organized strike-breaking can only be overcome by energetic co-ordinated organization. It will therefore be necessary before and especially during the struggle to strengthen the fractions (the revolutionary trade unions), to widen and strengthen the opposition by gradually consolidating organizationally our growing political influence. It is precisely during big struggles that all the organs of the Party, the trade union opposition and the revolutionary unions must work with the utmost intensity, drawing new sections of workers into energetic struggle against the strike-breaking methods of the reformists.

Thus only stubborn, systematic, strenuous work for the consolidation and welding together of our ranks will enable us to do away with blacklegging and to achieve a favourable issue to the struggle against the united front of the employers, the bourgeois State and the reformist trade union apparatus.

XII. STRIKES IN COUNTRIES WITH A DISRUPTED TRADE UNION MOVEMENT

The revolutionary unions in countries with a disrupted trade union movement (France, Czecho-Slovakia, Rumania, Greece, Japan, etc.), in addition to making use of the international political and tactical experiences in the industrial struggles, are confronted with a whole series of specific tasks, which become very acute when a mass movement is taking place. While in countries such as Germany and Great Britain the struggle for the leadership of the masses goes on between the official organ of the trade union and the opposition, in countries with a disrupted trade union movement it goes on between two organizations which are contesting for influence over the masses and leadership in the movement. In such a situation one of the most important tasks of the revolutionary unions is utilization of every industrial struggle in order to strengthen their own positions by widening the framework of the revolutionary unions through the capture of new members from the ranks of the unorganized at the expense of the reformist unions. During and immediately after the struggle everything should be done to liquidate the parallel reformist organization by getting all or an overwhelming majority of its members to join the ranks of the revolutionary unions (resolution of the IV Congress of the R.I.L.U. on the first item of the agenda). In this connection the effort made in Bordeaux during the dockers' strike deserves careful study and imitation, when the reformist union was reduced to nothing owing to its members going over to the unitarian union.

As to the reformist union in which only part of the members have been captured, during or immediately after the strike measures must be taken for the consolidation of our political and organization influence in them, in order to capture the majority of the members and to create thereby the premise for the smashing up of this reformist organization.

On the other hand, the existence of two parallel organizations demands of the revolutionary union special knowledge of the mood of the masses as well as struggle against the demagogy of the reformist leaders, who are prepared to simulate readiness to fight in order not to lose their influence on the rank-and-file members. In such countries it is particularly dangerous for the adherents of the R.I.L.U. to let the initiative be taken out of their hands, to be taken in by the Left phraseology of the reformist leaders, and to believe that the reformists are actually inclined and capable of struggling against the bourgeoisie. This would be the surest way of destroying the revolutionary trade union movement. If the local union belonging to the reformist centre is really carrying on a struggle against the employers it is naturally incumbent on the revolutionary union to establish a united front with it, but measures should be taken for the eventuality of capitulation moods, especially at the decisive moments of the struggle. The revolutionary union must get hold of the mass of the workers, those organized in the various unions as well as the unorganized, and must prove by deeds that the revolutionary union alone is working consistently in the interests of the workers. It is therefore essential for the revolutionary organization to rest on the elected strike committees and to collaborate with them as much as possible. It is only by a correct policy in the leadership of industrial struggles that the revolutionary unions can gain authority in the eyes of the masses, can consolidate them politically and organizationally and convert them into organizations embracing the majority of the working class.

XIII. STRIKES IN FASCIST AND WHITE TERROR COUNTRIES

Most of the strikes in Fascist and White Terror countries are spontaneous. This means that the adherents of the R.I.L.U. have been unable in these countries to penetrate into the enterprises in order to influence, in spite of reprisals, the demands and issue of a strike from its very beginning. This shows that for countries of this type work in the enterprises themselves is of particular importance, because they are the only place for economic and political sorties. In countries where bringing forward economic demands is considered a crime it is all the more necessary to bring them forward and to rally around them as many workers as possible. Demands should be drawn up in the factory departments and presented by a big delegation of 100 or 200 members. But this must not be considered a cast-iron rule for all countries. It must be, on the contrary, adapted to the special conditions of the various White Terror and Fascist countries. But under any circumstances the composition of the elected delegation must be such as not to expose the whole active trade union cadre to reprisals and terrorism. The election of delegates can and must be organized even in regard to the smallest question, if it concerns directly the interests of the workers. In these countries it is very important to appoint an efficient strike committee. When the election of the strike committee takes place one should bear in mind that arrests and reprisals must be expected. To provide for this contingency one should select a small leading group from the personnel of the big strike committee capable of taking upon itself the leadership of the strike in case of negotiations and persecutions. In these countries information and liaison is of particular importance, and this requires an illegal apparatus. Of great importance in these countries is protection of the strikers from the Fascist gangs, and for this purpose special self-defence corps should be organized. The main thing in these countries is to insist in every strike on open action, and to take advantage during the strike of every opportunity for emerging from the underground hiding place.

In view of the rapid fascization of the trade union movement in all the countries of Fascist dictatorship every industrial struggle brings home to the revolutionary trade union movement and the masses the necessity of sharper struggle against the Fascist agents in the trade union movement, the necessity of setting against the whole Fascist trade union system the revolutionary trade union organizations. Thus it is imperative to establish revolutionary trade unions in Poland and Hungary, to strengthen and develop them into mass organizations in Bulgaria and Rumania, to organize the workers in illegal revolutionary trade unions in Italy and Yugoslavia — everywhere in closest contact with the struggle for the legal existence of the proletarian class trade unions, against the terrorism of the Government and its agents in the trade union movement, against the Fascist dictatorship.

XIV HOW TO GIVE POLITICAL CONTENT TO STRIKES

Under the conditions of capitalist concentration, and in view of the tendency of the bourgeoisie and reformists to substitute compulsory arbitration for strikes, every strike assumes a political character. But this does not mean that all the workers understand the political, *i.e.,* the class, meaning of the industrial struggles which are going on. Under such circumstances it is incumbent on the adherents of the R.I.L.U. to teach the masses politics on the basis of the experiences of the daily struggles. Namely, it is necessary — on the basis of the general demands, which must not be lost sight of — to bring forward at every stage of the struggle slogans which raise the struggle to a higher plane. Converting strikes into political strikes does not mean talking nothing but politics; it means connecting immediate demands with those of a more general nature. For instance, most strikes meet with reprisals; the strikers get a taste of the compulsory arbitration system, and of black-legging under the protection of the authorities, etc. It is therefore clear that in every strike these questions must become fighting slogans. The main thing is for every worker to learn from the struggle that the State is protecting the employers against the workers, that "above class" justice, the press, Church, etc., are in the service of the employers, and that every big industrial conflict unrolls the problem of the "class against class" struggle. One should certainly not bring forward too many slogans all at once, bearing in mind that the most useful political slogan is that which is closely connected with the trend and incidents of the industrial conflict.

In this respect the political fighting slogans (demands) connected with the respective mass action of the proletariat can constitute in their entirety the united political platform on which the workers of all political shades of opinion, as well as non-party workers, can associate.

The fact that the masses are more active during strikes must be utilized by us TO STRENGTHEN THE WAR DANGER CAMPAIGN IN REGARD TO THE U.S.S.R. Every worker must be able to realize the close connection between the war preparations against the proletarian State and the accentuation of methods of exploitation, pressure and terrorism by which the capitalists oppress workers in the name of capitalist stabilization. During strikes the revolutionary trade union movement pays special attention to the mobilization of workers in enterprises connected with the war industry and of railwaymen. We must popularize among them the slogan of general strike, mass strike and suspension of transport during the war. In connection with the struggle against the imperialist war, we must struggle against all forms of militarization and formation of military organizations in the enterprises.

XV. FORMS AND METHODS OF MOBILIZATION OF TRADE UNION OPPOSITION THROUGHOUT THE COUNTRY

The experience of the recent strikes in France, Germany and Poland has shown that in times of strike the local organizations do not get the necessary help and support from the Party, the revolutionary trade unions and the trade union opposition, and yet active leadership in a serious industrial struggle on the part of the revolutionary unions and the trade union opposition is impossible unless we succeed in mobilizing all the forces at our disposal. Therefore the most important task of the revolutionary unions and the trade union opposition is:

1. As soon as a conflict is maturing in some branch of industry the best forces must be sent to the field of struggle.

2. The entire agitation and propaganda must be adapted to the significance and importance of the conflict.

3. The struggles are to be given a proper place in the press; the strikers themselves should be asked to contribute to the newspapers.

4. The whole work of the revolutionary unions and the trade union opposition should be at the service of the strike. The whole current work should be organized in a manner to give the fullest possible support to the strike.

5. The activity of every comrade entrusted with a definite branch of work must be strictly controlled.

6. Care should be taken that in times of strike new forces be drawn from the circles of men and women workers, adult and adolescent, of the respective branch of industry for all important work. It will be possible to find here hundreds and thousands of people who will do much useful work voluntarily.

7. A regular connection is to be established between the leading fighting organ and the central executive of the revolutionary trade union movement.

8. In order to mobilize all the forces in support of the struggle the trade unionists in direct charge of the conflict must give the central authority a correct idea of the state of affairs without trying to make things appear in a rosy light.

XVI. WORK AMONG WOMEN WORKERS AND WORKING
MEN'S WIVES

In view of the rationalization of industry and the extension of woman labour it is of particular importance to draw women workers into strikes. We have learned by experience that women workers and working men's wives play a very important rôle in strikes and lock-outs. Therefore the following is necessary:

1. Already during the preliminary work special attention should be paid to the organization of women workers and the inclusion of their special demands in the general demands.

2. During the strike women workers and working men's wives are to be drawn into active collaboration and entrusted with various functions in regard to agitation, organization and auxiliary service. For this purpose special working women's committees should be formed.

3. Special FLYING COLUMNS of women workers are to be formed for canvassing working men's wives.

4. When electing lock-out or strike committees care should be taken that they should include a considerable percentage of women

workers. In enterprises where women labour predominates women workers should be in a majority in the strike committees.

5. We must certainly have women workers as delegates to keep up the connection with other districts and branches of industry.

6. If a strike or lock-out affects a considerable number of women workers special women workers' conferences are to be called in order to prepare these women in an organized manner for the struggle and to get the most active among them elected to the strike committees. But this is on no account to preclude the participation of women workers in the general conferences together with their male colleagues.

As it frequently happens that the reformists settle conflicts at the expense of the weakest section of the proletariat (women and young workers), care should be taken at the conclusion of a conflict that the interests of these two categories of workers are looked after.

XVII. FORMS AND METHODS OF DRAWING THE YOUTH
INTO STRUGGLE

In times of industrial conflicts special attention should be paid to the protection of the interests of the youth and its inclusion in the struggle. When drawing up demands special points should be included referring to youth labour. When fighting organs are elected the youth must be considered as much as the adult workers. The youth can play a particularly important rôle in regard to picketing, self-defence "Hundreds," establishment of liaison, control over the carrying out of the decisions made by the leading organ, circulation of the literature of the strike committee, etc. A determined struggle must be waged against the Social-Democratic tradition that the youth is a category of workers to which no consideration is due. The adherents of the R.I.L.U. must bear in mind that the measure of the inclusion of young workers in the struggle will be to a great extent the measure of the activization of the whole movement.

It is advisable to form youth commissions in the strike committees for special work among the youth, in order to bring all young workers and apprentices into the strike front.

XVIII. ORGANIZATION OF FINANCIAL SUPPORT

The question of financial support during a strike plays a very important rôle. As the reformist unions are sabotaging the movement and are frequently declaring a strike unofficial in order not to give financial support to the strikers, and as the unorganized are ignored or repulsed by the reformists, who refuse to give them help of any kind, it is incumbent on the trade union opposition and the strike committee to raise as big funds as possible in order to come to the assistance of locked-out workers and strikers.

For this purpose it is necessary to act as follows:

1. The union is to be asked to give assistance to every striker and locked-out worker.

2. The union is to be asked to allow a definite sum as strike benefit for the unorganized.

3. Special collections of money are to be organized among the workers of the whole country in order to support the organized as well as the unorganized.

4. The Workers' International Relief, which is functioning as a relief organization in times of industrial struggle, is to be drawn into this work. In countries with an independent revolutionary trade union movement it is incumbent on the revolutionary unions to support the strikers. The local organizations of the W.I.R. are also to be drawn into this.

5. Special attention is to be paid to the utilization of co-operatives in times of industrial conflict; but to achieve this the opposition of the co-operative bureaucrats, who hold the view that lock-outs and strikes do not concern them, must be overcome.

6. In the municipal councils and parliaments demands should be brought forward for support for the workers affected by lockouts or strikes, and for their dependents. These demands should be

effectively supported by delegations and demonstrations of the workers engaged in the struggle.

XIX. INFORMATION AND LIAISON

One of the most important tasks during a strike or lock-out consists in establishing liaison between the elected organs and all those who participate in the struggle, and to keep everyone concerned fully informed about all developments connected with the struggle.

This requires:

1. Regular strike committee meetings and regular reports on its sessions to the participants of the struggle.

2. Rapid and current reporting in the press on the trend of the struggle and all important developments.

3. Publication of special newspapers or bulletins by the strike committees on the basis of a united class struggle platform. These organs should make regular reports on the trend of the struggle and the activity of the committees of action, as well as on the carrying out of the relief measures, etc.

4. Everything the bourgeois and reformist press writes about the struggles must be carefully followed and properly answered in the Labour press and in the bulletin of the strike committee.

5. Full use should be made of workers' sport leagues, such as cyclists, etc., in the interests of information and liaison. Sport is to be used in times of strike for the establishment and upkeep of liaison between the strikers of various enterprises or various districts.

XX. CONNECTIONS WITH BROTHER ORGANIZATIONS
OF OTHER COUNTRIES

Although the big struggles of the textile workers in North France, Münich-Gladbach and Lodz took place almost simultaneously, there was no contact between the strikers; and yet such liaison would have been very useful in these strikes. Therefore we must act in future as follows:

1. Establishment of connections with the workers of other districts and branches of industry through the election of special delegations.

2. In case of bigger conflicts it is desirable that the strike committees should approach the workers of other countries.

3. The international Press should be supplied with regular and full information about the trend of the strike and the methods of the struggle for publication abroad.

4. The Red International of Labour Unions and the Comintern must be systematically informed about all the details of the struggles.

5. The reformist unions and Internationals must be continually exposed because of their inactivity and hostility to the struggles.

XXI. CONCLUDING REMARKS

The decisions of the Eleventh Plenum of the E.C.C.I. and the V Congress of the R.I.L.U. concerning work in the reformist trade unions remain in force. As questions connected with industrial struggles are of interest to all Communist Parties, revolutionary trade unions and the revolutionary opposition, the Communist International and the Red International of Labour Unions, will on their part, carefully watch all industrial struggles; they will react at the right time to everything going on in this sphere in every country and will help to the best of their ability with the preparation and carrying through of the struggles. Such collaboration between the Comintern, the R.I.L.U. and their national Sections is the only means of making proper use of the industrial conflicts for the international Labour movement and of wresting the leadership of the masses from the hands of International Reformism."

Index, Bibliography and Guide to Further Reading

IN ADDITION to those books from which extracts are reprinted in the foregoing pages, we have consulted a large number of works, the more important of which are given below as a guide to further reading. A very full list of books and pamphlets on the history of British trade unionism is contained in R. & E. FROW and M. KATANKA, *The History of British Trade Unionism – A Select Bibliography* (Historical Assoc. 1969).

For the general reader the best works covering the whole of the period are COLE, G. D. H. *A Short History of the British Working Class Movement, 1789-1947* (Revised Edition, 1948) and WEBB, S. & B. *History of Trade Unionism* (Revised, 1920). Two books dealing in a more detailed way with industrial disputes are ASKWITH, G. R. *Industrial Problems and Disputes* (1920) and KNOWLES, K. G. J. C. *Strikes: a study in industrial conflict with special reference to British experience between 1911 and 1947* (1952).

224

227